IT'S YOUR MOVE

TOUGH PUZZLES

CHRIS WARD

EVERYMAN CHESS

Gloucester Publishers plc   www.everymanchess.com

First published in 2003 by Gloucester Publishers plc (formerly Everyman Publishers plc), Gloucester Mansions, 140A Shaftesbury Avenue, London WC2H 8HD

British Library Cataloguing-in-Publication Data
A catalogue record for this book is available from the British Library.

ISBN 1 85744 341 1

Distributed in North America by The Globe Pequot Press, P.O Box 480, 246 Goose Lane, Guilford, CT 06437-0480.

All other sales enquiries should be directed to Everyman Chess, Gloucester Publishers plc, Gloucester Mansions, 140A Shaftesbury Avenue, London WC2H 8HD. (tel: 020 7539 7600 fax: 020 7379 4060) email: info@everymanchess.com; website: www.everymanchess.com

To the Wood Green captain Brian Smith, whose hard work and desire helped make this book what it is.

EVERYMAN CHESS SERIES (formerly Cadogan Chess)
Chief Advisor: Garry Kasparov
Commissioning editor: Byron Jacobs

Typeset and edited by First Rank Publishing, Brighton.
Cover design by Horatio Monteverde.
Production by Navigator Guides.
Printed and bound in Great Britain by Biddles Ltd.

Contents

Introduction

So you're back, even though this time the puzzles are much tougher. Well good for you and I'm glad that you chose to join me and our panel on the adventure that is 'It's your move!'

The questions throughout this book are not just of the right/wrong variety and there are no checkmates in four or more! Most of the exercises will test your positional understanding of the game and if you don't have the required technique at the start then hopefully you will by the end!

In case you are new to this different type of quiz series, the story is as follows: you will be asked a question based on a position and you must decide which fictitious character is offering the most relevant answer. The panellists are:

'Analytical' Anatoly
Born and bred of the Russian chess school, they don't come much less emotional than Anatoly. He never makes a rash decision and any offering is based on pure calculation. He's good, really good, but um not that good because to let you into a little secret, he doesn't always select the best answer!

'Battling' Boris
Also originally from the ex-Soviet Union, Boris remembers his education in the chess schools of Moscow. Unfortunately, since leaving to live abroad his play appears to have been tainted by too many large open events and it possibly English weekend congresses too! He never shirks a challenge but you feel that some of his old teachers might be turning in their graves if they could see some of the rather radical solutions that he now provides.

'Creative' Chris
Chris is naturally talented, but probably chess is not where that talent lies! In all fairness, he often comes up with some fascinating ideas. However, there is a fine line between genius and over-elaboration and his chess plans

range from the sublime to the ridiculous. He could score ten points, he could score nought - you decide!

'Desperate' Dan

Desperate Dan comes right out of a comic book! He doesn't like hanging around or for that matter many other things! When it comes to chess he likes to win and he will do almost anything in order to achieve that goal. Even the kitchen sink will go into his attacks but he gets very moody if he doesn't win or is deprived the ability to wash his dishes!

'Elegant' Elizabeth

Everyone stops and stares when Elizabeth glides into the tournament hall and her play mirrors her demeanour. Graceful in her appearance and manner, her chess games can be equally stylish. Cool, calm and collected, she is the voice of reason. Unfortunately, the problem is that not everyone can speak her language!

Arguably some questions may be down to a matter of taste but I think that I've been fair in the marking scheme and points awarded are between 0 and 10. Make your selection, check the answer and then tot up your points. Consulting the chart at the back will then tell you how you have performed.

The vast majority of these questions are based on real encounters and many are from famous matches. I would like to thank my fellow British League Wood Green team-mates for their wonderful contribution to this book. As the wine flowed at last season's victory celebration dinner, I was fortunate enough to have the likes of Grandmasters Michael Adams, Nigel Short, Jon Speelman, Alex Baburin, Bogdan Lalic, Matthew Turner and John Emms suggesting examples from chess history that stuck in their minds as extraordinary or especially instructive plans. FIDE Master Peter Sowray was also a fantastic source of information and quite frankly put my own knowledge of the old classics to shame. While I like to think that I did extra work besides, this book is the culmination of that May evening.

Enjoy!

Chris Ward,
Kent,
September 2003

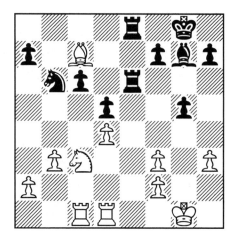

Position after 22 gxf3

Black to play
Let's start with an easy one! Black dominates the e-file and has an obvious structural advantage, particularly bearing in mind White's shattered kingside. From this position of strength, how should he set about making progress?

Anatoly
Anatoly has calculated that Black can win a pawn pretty much by force. It's a long procedure which involves doubling the rooks on the h-file to hit the isolated h-pawn. Starting with 22...♖h6, by parking one of the two on h4, White's d-pawn also comes under scrutiny. With a switch to the f-file also possible, White will find it impossible to hold his position together.

Boris
Boris wants to allow all of his pieces to get in on the act. The king is a valuable piece in endings and he wants to prepare its introduc-

tion via 22...f5. White can only sit and watch as Black continues to improve his position.

Chris
Chris wants to manoeuvre his knight to somewhere useful and with e7 or d6 as possible stop-offs, he sees the f5-square as an ideal location. From there it will add further pressure to the isolani on d4 and perhaps even spring to h4 in order to attack f3. His preferred move here is 22...♘c8.

Dan
Characteristically, Dan is desperate to get his knight into the game too but instead believes 22...♘d7 to be best. With bigger fish to fry later, he likes the idea of even temporarily controlling the e5- and c5-squares and doesn't fancy retreating his steed to the back rank.

Elizabeth
Not convinced as to which route the black knight should take, Elizabeth is more with Boris for the time being. The fundamental difference is that she favours 22...h5 in order to facilitate a king entry via h7. She believes her method has the advantage of not depriving one of her pieces of the f5-square.

☐ Anatoly	☐ Boris	☐ Chris	☐ Dan	☐ Elizabeth

Points: ....

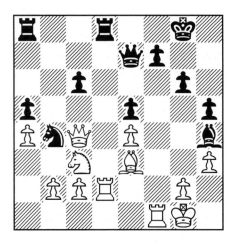

Position after 23...罝fd8

White to play
One feels that White should have the advantage here as he has the better bishop and is generally more centralised. The knight on b4 is a bit of a nuisance, though. How should White deal with that particular problem?

Anatoly
Anatoly has plumped for the bizarre-looking 24 ♘b1. His reasoning is that there is no need to panic into trading off Black's well placed steed and instead threatens to force it back to a significantly inferior square via c2-c3. His belief, based on concrete analysis, is that his own knight will later re-emerge via d2 and probably f3.

Boris
For Boris it is 24 罝fd1 that suggests itself. He is loath to vacate the half-open f-file as there is already some handy pressure against f7. However, as the d-file is completely open, to him it

makes sense to furiously contest it.

Regarding the specific question of the b4-knight, his suspicion is that patience is the name of the game.

Chris

Chris is subscribing to the view that when you have a space advantage you should avoid fair swaps, and he is opting for 24 ♖e2. The d-file entry points are all covered and his aim is ultimately to double his rooks on the f-file. Similarly, he isn't too worried about Black's knight just yet and will deal with that situation further down the line.

Dan

There is no hanging around for Dan! He likes 24 ♗c5 and, after trading rooks, has every intention of swapping the pieces that in his opinion will leave him with a good knight against a bad bishop and in all likelihood a passed a-pawn too.

Elizabeth

For Elizabeth the answer is simple. She prefers to preserve her bishop and instead likes the idea of 24 ♘a2. It is a standard policy to trade your poorly placed pieces for your opponent's well placed ones and for her this dinky knight retreat fits the bill nicely.

☐ Anatoly ☐ Boris	☐ Chris	☐ Dan	☐ Elizabeth
Points:			

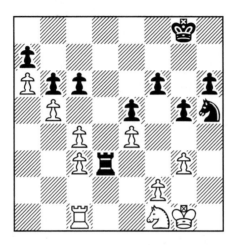

Position after 33...♘xh5

White to play
Visually White appears to be on the back foot here; in fact all of his pieces are on the back rank and an enemy rook has infiltrated his position. That said, Black's knight is offside and another saving grace for White could be his dangerously advanced queenside pawn majority. How should White handle this situation?

Anatoly
The calculations have been made and Anatoly's conclusion is that 34 ♖b1 wins practically by force. To avoid big time tactics on b6 Black must seal up the queenside with 34...c5, but then the white knight springs to e3 and thus inevitably d5 to devastating effect.

Boris
Boris would like to activate his rook as quickly as possible but understands that it must bide its time for now. Instead 34 ♘e3 is a must. From there the knight would have some strong options and

♖d1, challenging the open file, becomes a reality.

Chris
Chris can see a tactical flaw in 34 ♘e3 and instead has discovered the sneaky 34 ♘h2. He will activate his king shortly but has made turning his knight into a menace more of a priority.

Dan
As usual Dan is desperate for action and, as it happens, thinks that White is spoilt for choice. Having analysed the position thoroughly, he believes that not only is White not struggling but in fact both 34 bxc6 and 34 c5 lead to swift victories.

Elizabeth
Elizabeth agrees with Chris about the tactical deficiencies of 34 ♘e3 but believes that White must keep his (or her!) nerve. White must stand firm with 34 ♔g2. Black is not threatening anything and so ♘e3 (the best place for the knight) can follow shortly.

☐ Anatoly	☐ Boris	☐ Chris	☐ Dan	☐ Elizabeth
Points:				

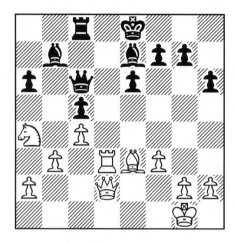

Position after 23...♚e8

White to play
You are White in the above position. Whose view to you think is the most appropriate regarding the assessment of this position and what to do?

Anatoly
Anatoly's belief is that Black's queenside pawn weaknesses are counterbalanced by his bishop pair advantage. Objectively there is no way to try to progress without making concessions. A move like 24 ♕f2 looks sensible and with no side realistically able to make progress (Black must continue to guard his isolated c-pawn), a friendly draw would be a fair result.

Boris
Boris refuses to believe that there is nothing doing here. In fact he is looking at an infiltration on d6 with his bishop via 24 ♗f4. His logic is that White can eliminate one of Black's bishop pair this way,

and by trading off pieces Black's isolated pawns become even more vulnerable.

Chris

Chris believes that the white knight could do better for itself than have the sole purpose of hitting c5. His view is that White has a slight edge, with the first priority being a relocation of the offside knight to pastures greener. Black isn't going anywhere and so a knight manoeuvre to the kingside (starting with 24 ♘c3) seems very reasonable.

Dan

Dan feels that with both kings on the kingside, one of White's advantages is a queenside pawn majority. He proposes taking the bull by the horns regarding a creation of a passed pawn. He likes the immediate 24 a3 with the intention of angling towards b3-b4.

Elizabeth

Although White is generally well centralised and that is usually a good thing, Elizabeth's recommendation is 24 ♕a5. She plans an invasion of Black's weak queenside and specifically the b6-square. It is her opinion that White is comfortably better and things should fall into place from there.

☐ Anatoly ☐ Boris ☐ Chris ☐ Dan ☐ Elizabeth

Points: ....

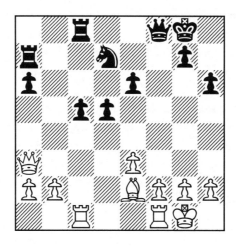

Position after 19...fxe6

White to play
All players in our panel have a justification for the move that they would play with White here. Whose story do you buy?

Anatoly
Thematic is 20 f4 according to Anatoly, who advocates creating an outpost on e5 and more importantly fixing the odd black pawn on the same colour as White's bishop.

Boris
Not beating about the bush, Boris wants to get to grips with Black's pawn structure immediately via 20 e4. As Black has more pawn islands than his opponent, structurally he is worse off. However, Boris thinks that White can create still more chinks in the armour.

Chris
Chris recommends 20 b4. As with Boris's idea, this also tackles

Black's pawn structure. This time, though, White ultimately seeks to gain control of the d4-square (as well as e5).

Dan
Dan likes the overall feel of White's position but sees a particular window of opportunity. It looks like a hot pawn but he has calculated that 20 ♗xa6 is in fact sound. A pawn is a pawn!

Elizabeth
Elizabeth's proposal is far less radical. She believes that there is no hurry and White should build up slowly. She wants to be ready to respond to any black threats but with the eventual aim of turning the pressure up on Black's c- and d-pawns. For now, though, 20 b3 will prevent ...c5-c4 and will offer the queen an access square back to the kingside.

☐ Anatoly ☐ Boris ☐ Chris ☐ Dan ☐ Elizabeth
Points: ....

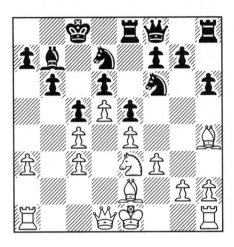

Position after 17...♕f8

White to play
White has a space advantage in this closed, typically 'Nimzo-Indian' middlegame. Which of our panel's plans would you recommend?

Anatoly
Anatoly believes that the queenside is in all likelihood going to be sealed off and hence the kingside is going to be where the action is. He advocates 18 0-0 and an ultimate plan of engineering the pawn break f3-f4. There will be hard work in arranging this but when achieved it will either provide him with a big centre or a half-open (or fully open) f-file.

Boris
As far as Boris is concerned the correct plan sticks out like a sore thumb! The white king need not commit itself just yet and so there is no need to wait. Yes, it's 18 a4 for Boris, who given the chance will advance the pawn again on the next turn. The main focus of

White's attention should be the a- and b-files.

Chris
Chris likes the move 18 ♕b1. His idea is a crafty bishop manoeuvre: ♗e2-d1-a4-c6. Only then will he start rolling the a-pawn down the board.

Dan
Dan feels that the important move here is 18 ♗xf6. His view is that in closed positions knights are more often better than bishops. If this trade is not made, Black will hunt the bishop down with annoying moves such as ...g7-g5. After the expected 18...♘xf6 White will 'patch up' the dark squares with 19 ♕d2 and then castle queenside. His king will be very safe over there and then he can get on with the real battle: the kingside.

Elizabeth
Elizabeth anticipates advancing her a-pawn (to ultimately pressurise the enemy monarch) but has the dinky 18 ♔d2 in mind. This useful waiting move helps to connect her rooks, and the key point is that with a closed centre, the white monarch will be perfectly safe in the middle.

☐ Anatoly	☐ Boris	☐ Chris	☐ Dan	☐ Elizabeth

Points: ....

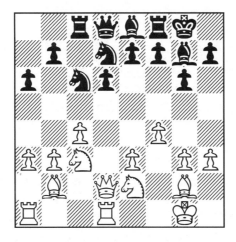

Position after 17...♛d8

White to play
Black's pieces look a little cramped and no doubt he dreams of breaking free with the likes of ...d6-d5 or ...b7-b5. How should White take his space advantage to the next level?

Anatoly
Anatoly has foreseen that although ...d6-d5 is a long way off for Black, the break ...b7-b5 is a very realistic possibility. Often a plan in itself is restricting your opponent's play and that is why he is plumping for 18 a4.

Boris
Boris is tempted by the natural 18 ♖ac1 but doesn't quite feel the need to commit this rook just yet. Instead he wants to get straight to the point with 18 g4. With Black's pieces poorly coordinated, his belief is that, with ♘g3 and f4-f5 likely follow-ups, a kingside attack is perfectly justifiable.

Chris

Chris wants to slowly push his opponent off the board. He favours the squeezing advance e3-e4 but has noted that it is tactically flawed just now. Instead he is happy with the preparatory 18 ♔h2.

Dan

Dan also wants to focus on the centre and he desires immediate confrontation in the form of 18 ♘d5. Although typically one avoids fair swaps when in possession of a space advantage, he wants to exchange dark-squared bishops and then take advantage of the weakened a1-h8 diagonal.

Elizabeth

Elizabeth likes her pawn on e3 and wants to put it to good use where it stands. She prefers turning up the heat another notch with a different knight move. Yes, it is 18 ♘d4 for her, the intention being to focus more on the g2-b7 diagonal than the b2-g7 one.

☐ Anatoly ☐ Boris ☐ Chris ☐ Dan ☐ Elizabeth

Points: ....

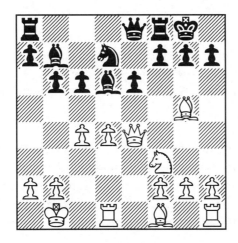

Position after 13...♛e8

White to play
Attack is often the name of the game in opposite side castling positions. Who do you think has the best move and accompanying explanation for White?

Anatoly
Anatoly believes that the most obvious move must be the best here. He can't see any justification for holding back on 14 ♗d3. Either Black then makes a concession in the fortress around his king with 14...g6 or else he concedes an outpost on e5 and a backward pawn on e6 via 14...f5.

Boris
Boris thinks that something extra is required and 14 h4 is just his cup of tea. This h-pawn could be employed in an attack itself, and in addition the option is there for the h1-rook to enter the game via h3.

Chris

Not the most obvious move, Chris has come up with 14 ♖e1. His justification is that it keeps Black's f-pawn in place, thus adding bite to the inevitable ♗d3.

Dan

Dan is desperate to keep Black's b7-bishop out of the equation and has thus come up with the intriguing sequence 14 c5 bxc5 15 ♗d3, which even after 15...f5 he believes is easily worth a pawn.

Elizabeth

Elizabeth appreciates the attraction of all the other panel members' suggestions but upon reflection has dismissed them all in favour of the controlling 14 ♘e5. She suggests that it's almost as though the knight is being pulled to that square by invisible forces, and to her it just feels like a gap that needs to be plugged.

☐ Anatoly ☐ Boris ☐ Chris ☐ Dan ☐ Elizabeth

Points: ....

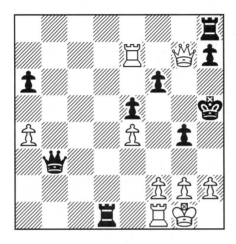

Position after 35...♖d1

White to play

This is one to get the grey matter working. White appears to have his opponent's king on the ropes, but with his monarch under some pressure too, all may not be as it seems. Who has the correct assessment of this position?

Anatoly

White should play 36 h3 here according to Anatoly. This gives his king a vital niche and following this, mate or a favourable endgame is inevitable.

Boris

We all know that Boris loves battling but he recommends caution here. His suggestion is 36 ♕f7+ leading to a double rook ending that, thanks to his seventh rank posting, should leave him with a comfortable edge.

Chris

Chris believes that White can cleverly prevent a perpetual check via the quiet move 36 ♖d7. This limits Black's checking potential but leaves White's queen in a menacing position.

Dan

Dan advocates striking whilst the iron is hot. Consequently he has turned to 36 ♖xe5+ and, put bluntly, believes that it is a forced win.

Elizabeth

Failing to find a win, Elizabeth wants to give her own king some breathing space. Her conclusion is that 36 g3 is the most accurate response. This allows Black a draw by perpetual which she suggests Black is seriously advised to take.

☐ Anatoly ☐ Boris   ☐ Chris   ☐ Dan   ☐ Elizabeth

Points: ....

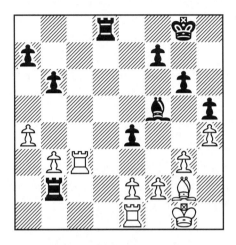

Position after 35 ♖c3

Black to play
The relative positioning of the rooks offer Black an advantage but often in endings a certain accuracy is required. Who in your opinion convinces you of the best move for Black here?

Anatoly
For Anatoly there is nothing to consider. Rooks love open files and they love doubling up. With this in mind, 35...♖bd2 is logical. Black dominates one of the open files and prepares the ...♖d1 challenge that would enable a further penetration.

Boris
Boris agrees that rooks like doubling up but suggests that as they also like the seventh rank, it is 25...♖dd2 that offers the best of both worlds!

Chris

Chris feels that White is tied up as it is and wants to advance his queenside pawns to more threatening positions. In particular he rates 35...a6, intending ...b6-b5 and the chance to embarrass the defensive white rook on c3 with ...b5-b4.

Dan

Dan wants his queenside pawn majority as quickly as possibly. Hence he favours 35...♗e6 in order to trade his e-pawn for White's b-pawn.

Elizabeth

Elizabeth's smooth idea is to improve the positioning of her d8-rook via the manoeuvre 35...♖d4 and ...♖b4. This would pile unbearable pressure on White's b-pawn.

□ Anatoly	□ Boris	□ Chris	□ Dan	□ Elizabeth
Points:				

Now turn to page 107 for the solutions to Test 1

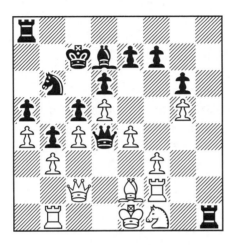

Position after 26 ☖f2

Black to play
In the above position Black is clearly on top as he has a superbly placed queen and rook. How should he go about turning the necessary screws in order to put his opponent away?

Anatoly
Anatoly knows that Black must bring more pieces into play in order to build on his advantage. The obvious move for him is 26...☖ah8, which of course does just that.

Boris
Boris wants to activate the a8-rook too but sees 26...f6 as best. Ultimately he is looking to open either the e- or the f-file.

Chris
Chris has the outrageous suggestion of 26...♛h8. Although he doesn't deny that her majesty is well placed in the centre, his idea

is that there are more rewards for it to reap on h4.

Dan

Dan feels that his minor pieces aren't pulling their weight and has just the solution. He has investigated the (possibly double piece) sacrifice 26...♘xa4 27 bxa4 ♗xa4. White's queen will be deflected, enabling Black to turn up the heat big time.

Elizabeth

A simple plan from Elizabeth. She believes that the black steed could pull its weight more and, not buying into the sacrifice on a4, she prefers the move 26...♗e8. Although temporarily a bad square for the bishop, this paves the way for a ...♘d7-e5 manoeuvre.

☐ Anatoly ☐ Boris   ☐ Chris   ☐ Dan   ☐ Elizabeth

Points: ....

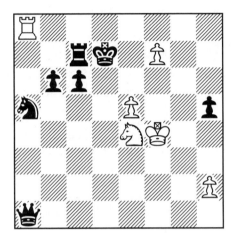

Position after 54...a1♕

White to play
In case you were feeling sleepy, here's a tactical one. Which of our panel knows what is going on in this position?

Anatoly
'It's easy' declares Anatoly. White forces checkmate through 55 ♖d8+.

Boris
Boris agrees that it is mate, but only by utilising an under-promotion.

Chris
Chris can't see a winning combination with the rook, pawn and knight but believes that he has hit the jackpot with 55 ♔f5. The king is a useful piece in the endgame, so use it!

Dan

Dan is up for going 'all in'. He's not sure about the kitchen sink, but he's only too pleased to offer the e-pawn and believes that White wins with 55 e6+.

Elizabeth

Elizabeth is a realist! She doesn't think that the checks come to anything whereas 55 f8♕ forces Black to enter an endgame with approximately equal chances. For her that is easily the best practical try.

☐ Anatoly   ☐ Boris   ☐ Chris   ☐ Dan   ☐ Elizabeth

Points: ....

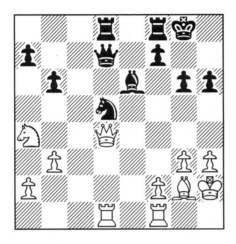

Position after 21...♖ad8

White to play

With all things considered the above position may appear fairly level. However, are there any weak features in Black's position that White can seek to exploit?

Anatoly

Anatoly thinks not and would thus prefer to concentrate on improving the position of his own pieces. Specifically the offside placing of the knight bugs him and hence his liking for the move 22 ♘b2. The steed can aim for e5 via c4 or d3.

Boris

Boris thinks that more direct confrontation is required and the move 22 ♘c3 is staring him in the face. According to him it is vital that Black isn't given time to escape the critical pin on the d-file. Note that with bishops on the board, Boris would happily take a queen over two rooks.

Chris

Chris likes 22 f4. Whilst this places a pawn on an active post working in tandem with the bishop (they cover different coloured squares), the ultimate aim is to advance it still further. This exploits the precarious positioning of the e6-bishop as well as the slightly weakened black kingside pawn structure - the pawns on h6 and g6.

Dan

Dan sees a big hole on f6 and wants his knight there. Generally he accepts that bishops are better than knights in open positions but here he proposes 22 ♗xd5 with the idea being to withdraw his knight to more central duties.

Elizabeth

Elizabeth wonders why people try to be clever when a sensible move will do fine. 22 ♕h4 is her preference. This attacks the pawn on h6 and uncovers the rook, making the d-file pin more worrying.

☐ Anatoly	☐ Boris	☐ Chris	☐ Dan	☐ Elizabeth

Points: ....

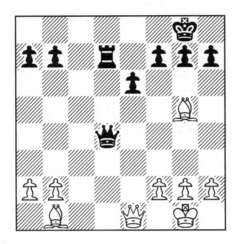

Black to play

Material-wise Black isn't doing that well in the above position (most would prefer two bishops to a rook and a pawn). If he can't find anything better he probably ought to grab the b2-pawn. However, bearing in mind potential back rank tricks, can you uncover which of our panel has a better solution?

Anatoly

Anatoly wants to set the ball rolling with 1...♕a4 with for now the most basic threat of 2...♖d1.

Boris

Boris similarly wants to get his rook down to d1 but prefers to kick off with 1...♕g4, which simultaneously attacks the g5-bishop.

Chris

Chris wants to conjure up something starting with the cheeky

1...♛b4. A visual start seeing as the queen is immune from capture.

Dan
Dan wants to employ the same theme as Chris, only he reckons that it is 1...♛e5 that puts Black on the road to victory.

Elizabeth
Elizabeth applauds the stylishness of the boys' attempts but finds it amusing that they have concentrated on the crazier moves when in fact it is the most blatant that hits gold. Her opinion is that Black can force the win of material via 1...♛d1.

☐ Anatoly ☐ Boris ☐ Chris ☐ Dan ☐ Elizabeth

Points: ....

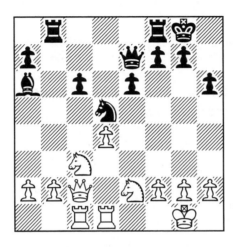

Position after 18...♕xe7

White to play
Which of our panel's candidate moves do you rate the most in the above position?

Anatoly
Anatoly has calculated many variations in which the already well placed black knight on d5 can cause problems. Hence he advocates 19 ♘xd5 and after 19...cxd5 suggests that White is slightly better due to the knight versus 'bad' bishop imbalance and queenside pawn majority.

Boris
Boris also believes that Black's bishop isn't as good as a knight in this particular position and, primarily in order to prevent the trade, recommends 19 ♘g3.

Chris
Chris sees a good window of opportunity for 19 ♘a4. This unleashes some of White's major pieces against Black's weak isolated c-pawn and prepares to occupy the outpost on c5.

Dan
Dan is eager to go on the offensive and doesn't like the way he is being tied down to the defence of the b2-pawn. He is torn between 19 ♖d2 and 19 b3 and plumps for the former because it doesn't weaken the c3- and a3-squares.

Elizabeth
Elizabeth really doesn't want to trade knights on d5 but with that in mind deems it necessary to control the b4-square. In her opinion 19 a3 is a very useful move.

☐ Anatoly ☐ Boris   ☐ Chris   ☐ Dan   ☐ Elizabeth

Points: ....

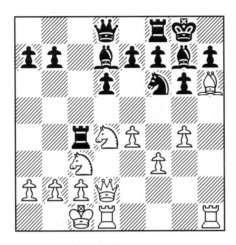

Position after 16 ♗h6

Black to play

It's a bit mean of me putting a Dragon in as surely there shouldn't be an opening theory bias! Well, this is an old line and I thought that it would get you thinking!

Anyway, White has just played 16 ♗h6 to reach the above position. He now appears to be threatening to bash his way down the h-file and deliver mate with the use of the f6-knight remover ♘d5. Perhaps Black should act quickly! Who has the best suggestion?

Anatoly

Anatoly favours 16...e6. This cuts out ♘d5 for good and the only drawback is the weakening of the d6-pawn. However, Black is already a pawn up and in the time it takes White to pick up that pawn, Black will develop counterplay elsewhere.

Boris

Boris likes 16...♗xh6 17 ♕xh6 ♖xc3. Black already has a pawn for this traditional Dragon exchange sacrifice, and the crippled queen-side pawns that White will be saddled with is another bonus.

Chris
Chris has investigated 16...♞xe4, unleashing an attack against the knight on d4. This is the best solution and in one line he even has this knight returning to f6 to save the day.

Dan
Dan recommends punishing White for a lack of protection of the knight on d4 and wants to expose this with the immediate 16...♜xd4.

Elizabeth
There is no need to panic providing Black can generate enough action of her own according to Elizabeth. She proposes 16...♛a5 in order to give White something to think about.

☐ Anatoly ☐ Boris ☐ Chris ☐ Dan ☐ Elizabeth

Points: ....

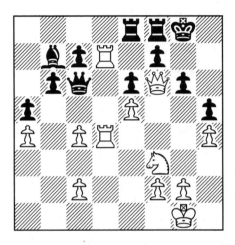

Position after 30...h5

White to play
White may have some weak queenside pawns but that aside his opponent appears to be completely tied up. How might he set about driving a nail through the coffin?

Anatoly
Anatoly has no hesitation in opting for 31 g4. He plans to open up the black king like a can of worms and believes that it is all plain sailing from there onwards.

Boris
With a similar intention of introducing his h-pawn into the attack, Boris has come up with the stunning 31 ♖g4. Upon 31...hxg4 32 h5, he has concluded that Black must concede significant material or else face the wrath of the most deadly attacking combination: the queen and the knight.

Chris

Chris understands that Black's only threat comes along the b7-g2 diagonal and, that aside, Black can do very little. His plan kicks off with 31 ♘e1 and involves a future f2-f3 and g2-g4. There will be no defence to the advance of White's kingside pawns.

Dan

Dan assesses that Black is particularly weak on the dark squares. White dominates the d-file but for him that is not enough. 31 ♖d8 is Dan's recommendation because without the rooks, the white queen and knight pairing will come into its own.

Elizabeth

Elizabeth has a very simple plan. All of the other pieces are accounted for and, although unusual, she wants to bring her king into the attack. She sees the manoeuvre 31 ♔h2 followed by ♔g3-f4-g5-h6 as a practically unstoppable idea to help deliver mate with the queen on g7.

☐ Anatoly ☐ Boris ☐ Chris ☐ Dan ☐ Elizabeth

Points: ....

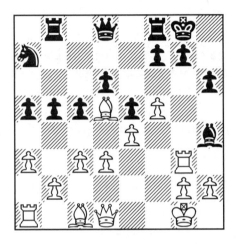

Position after 19...♗h4

White to play
White has a lovely bishop pair and a generous space advantage courtesy of the advanced pawn on f5. Surely White has several good possibilities, but how would you deal with the attack on the g3-rook?

Anatoly
20 ♕h5 is the best move according to Anatoly, who after 20...♗xg3 21 hxg3 can see no satisfactory defence to pushing a g-pawn (or perhaps even two!) up the board.

Boris
Boris believes that 20 ♖g6 is the most accurate continuation. White's bishops are amazingly powerful and he likes the idea of utilising the pin on the f7-pawn.

Chris

Only minimal creation here: '20 ♕g4 gets straight to the point' says Chris, who obviously has the intention of meeting 20...♗xg3 with 21 ♗xh6.

Dan

Dan can see Chris's way of thinking but doesn't understand the need to hang around when 20 ♗xh6 is just crying out to be played.

Elizabeth

Elizabeth sees no need to be clever particularly when 20 ♖h3 is both safe and strong.

☐ Anatoly ☐ Boris ☐ Chris ☐ Dan ☐ Elizabeth

Points: ....

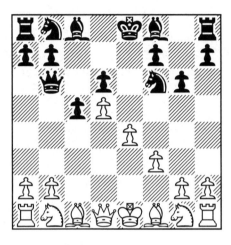

Position after 10...g6

White to play
White is yet to develop any pieces in the above position but now is his chance. It's fair to say that often the choice of squares for any given piece may be purely down to a matter of taste. Whose recommended piece set-up most appeals to you?

Anatoly
White should play 11 ♘c3 and then follow that up shortly with ♗c4, ♘ge2 and 0-0. It will later become clear where the c1-bishop should be called into action.

Boris
Boris agrees that White should kick off with 11 ♘c3 but, after the anticipated 11...♗g7, he has something a little different in mind. He wants to go with his kingside pawns. Yes, with the black queen a little offside he fancies 12 g4 with the aim of following up with h4-h5. If Black castles short then there is an obvious kingside attack

and if he doesn't then White will be in control of the tension there anyway.

Chris

Chris wants to post his knights on their best positions. He acknowledges that one must go to c3 but is advocating 11 ♘e2-c3 to solve that problem. His intention is to locate the other on c4 and implies that sooner or later it can get there via d2 or more likely a3.

Dan

Dan wants to castle kingside. However, although he plumps for 11 ♘c3 now, he would prefer the other knight on f3. Thus he is intending to advance his f-pawn at least one more square in the near future to facilitate ♘g1-f3 and offer both e4-e5 and f4-f5 possibilities in the future.

Elizabeth

Not having brought out any pieces yet, Elizabeth has spotted the opportunity to challenge the a1-h8 diagonal immediately. Hence 11 b3, when intended follow-up moves include ♗b2, ♘d2, ♕c2, ♗d3 and ♘e2. Then the option is there to castle on either side.

☐ Anatoly ☐ Boris ☐ Chris ☐ Dan ☐ Elizabeth

Points: ....

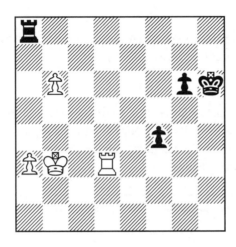

Position after 45...f4

White to play

White has the initiative here because his set of connected passed pawns is further advanced than his opponent's. Once you get involved in this position, though, you will discover that it is not as easy as one might think. Who has the best plan to help see White victorious?

Anatoly

Rooks belong behind passed pawns, but in direct contravention of that rule Anatoly is advocating 46 ♖f3. White's rook can hold up the black pawns but its enemy number won't have such luck with those on the a- and b-files.

Boris

Boris thinks that Anatoly is speaking rubbish. For him, pushing the passed pawns as quickly as possible must be the best solution - hence 46 a4.

Chris

Chris wants to tie the black rook down immediately, and after 46 b7 ♖b8 47 ♖d7 the a-pawn can stroll up the board unimpeded.

Dan

Dan is very keen on kings in endgames and thus favours 46 ♔b4, intending to meet 46...g5 with 47 ♔c5.

Elizabeth

Elizabeth's intriguing plan starts with 46 ♔c2 and involves recalling the king to help stop Black's pawns. Its enemy number is too far away to successfully accomplish the same with White's pawns and that is the decisive factor.

☐ Anatoly	☐ Boris	☐ Chris	☐ Dan	☐ Elizabeth

Points: ....

Now turn to page 127 for the solutions to Test 2

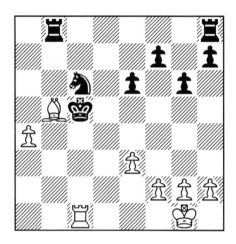

Position after 29 ♖c1+

Black to play
Black is the exchange for a pawn up but must now pick a square for his checked king. Should there be a preference?

Anatoly
Not according to Anatoly. His opinion is that any of the legal moves should win as the material advantage is significant.

Boris
Boris believes that the black monarch should remain centralised. His preference is for 29...♚d5 30 ♗xc6+ ♚e5.

Chris
Chris isn't too worried about the placing of the black king but is more concerned about trading off a pair of rooks. He believes that this is best achieved via 29...♚b4.

Dan

Dan goes for 29...♚d6 30 ♖xc6+ ♚e7 as it is his belief that the black king should stay with the pawns and the black rooks should go out on the hunt.

Elizabeth

Elizabeth rates 29...♚b6 30 ♖xc6+ ♚b7 as best. The black monarch is there to halt White's passed pawn, and the added bonus is that Black can then trade off a pair of rooks on the c- or d-file.

☐ Anatoly ☐ Boris ☐ Chris ☐ Dan ☐ Elizabeth

Points: ....

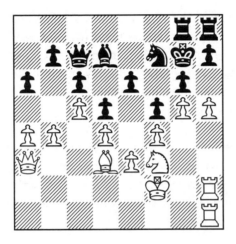

Position after 35...⃞bg8

White to play
White has a tremendous space advantage in the position above and obviously a much better bishop. Who has the most convincing plan for turning these pluses into a full point?

Anatoly
Anatoly likes the idea of sealing off the queenside. This prevents any counterplay on that side of the board, leaving him free to concentrate his efforts on the kingside. After 36 a5 he would treble up his major pieces on the h-file in preparation for an inevitable invasion on h7.

Boris
Boris feels that although White has the initiative on both sides of the board, the main action is going to be in the centre. Following 36 h6+ ♔f8 White intends angling for an e3-e4 break. This will obviously involve a piece sacrifice but with Black's pieces so uncoordi-

nated, a major piece build-up on the e-file for White will be devastating.

Chris
Chris wants to retain the tension in the position and has great plans for the h-file. His preferred continuation is 36 ♖h4. He would then nudge the other rook up before bringing the queen behind them. His view differs from Anatoly's mainly in his belief that 36 a5 is both unnecessary and indeed a mistake.

Dan
Dan is desperate for major piece action but although the attraction of the h-file is obvious, he favours an infiltration on the queenside. He likes 36 b5 and intends meeting 36...axb5 with 37 h6+ ♔f8 38 axb5 followed by what he believes will be a decisive entry into his opponent's position via the a-file.

Elizabeth
Elizabeth believes that the rest of the panel are overlooking Black's own threats: Black is intending to unleash ...h7-h6. Thus 36 hxg6 hxg6 and a trade of all the rooks must be the way to go before her other break b4-b5 is employed.

□ Anatoly	□ Boris	□ Chris	□ Dan	□ Elizabeth

Points: ....

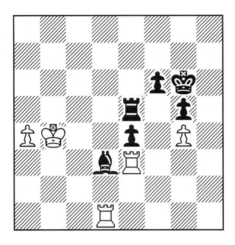

Position after 40...♗d3

White to play
Yes, it's another two rooks versus rook, bishop and pawn scenario but is White really better in this one? Who do you trust?

Anatoly
Be warned as Anatoly spent an awful long time over this position, eventually concluding that White is winning but only with 41 a5.

Boris
Boris disagrees with Anatoly's suggestion and instead proposes eliminating Black's powerful bishop via 41 ♖exd3 (or ♖dxd3) exd3 42 ♖xd3. Due to his outside passed pawn, White stands better but is in all likelihood not winning.

Chris
Chris believes that White has excellent winning chances after 41 ♖a1 as in his opinion the white king is offered more options. Spe-

cifically, when the a-pawn advances next turn, it won't be driven to the a-file and will instead be able if needed to return to the kingside to keep an eye on black's pawns.

Dan
Dan thinks that actually this position is really easy. 'It's come straight out of a simple puzzle book!' he exclaims, with the solution being 42 ♖dxd3 exd3 43 ♖xe5. With the white king returning to stop the pawns, it's game, set and match!

Elizabeth
Elizabeth is of the opinion that a rook and bishop combine very well together in the endgame. Despite the material difference, she believes that this endgame is in fact fairly unclear. Essentially her conclusion is that there are a number of sensible moves that White might make here with the most likely outcome being a draw.

☐ Anatoly ☐ Boris ☐ Chris ☐ Dan ☐ Elizabeth

Points: ....

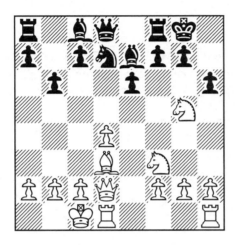

Position after 11...h6

White to play
Not long out of the opening, the above depicts a position of opposite-side castling. With White to move, who do you think tenders the most attractive continuation?

Anatoly
Anatoly likes 12 ♗h7+. This forces the king into the corner and that is useful for when White later rolls his (or her) kingside pawns down the board.

Boris
Possibly with similar ideas in mind, Boris favours the immediate 12 h4, believing that Black grabs the g5-knight at his peril.

Chris
Chris prefers a knight relocation. He is all for 12 ♘h3, preparing to bring the steed to the handy square f4.

Dan

Dan wants to go 'in like Flynn'. 12 ♘h7 ♖e8 13 g4, with excellent prospects for a successful kingside attack, is the sequence that he is game for.

Elizabeth

Elizabeth's opinion is that the g5-knight has done its job of provoking a weakness in the enemy defensive pawn shield and is more than happy, for the time being at least, to return it to e4.

☐ Anatoly ☐ Boris   ☐ Chris   ☐ Dan   ☐ Elizabeth

Points: ....

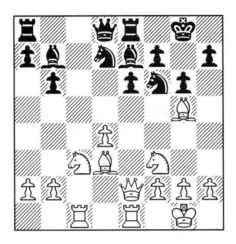

Position after 14...g6

White to play
With White to play here, which move and associated plan rings your chimes?

Anatoly
Anatoly suggests 15 a4. White is well placed in the centre and now wants to get a grip on the queenside.

Boris
Boris prefers the mirror image, 16 h4. A kingside attack is typical in an 'Isolated Queen's Pawn' situation such as this and he wants to get to grips with that g6 blockade.

Chris
Chris feels that in general White should want to preserve pieces but is attracted to 16 ♗a6. His logic is that if he can remove the b7-bishop then the c6-square will be there for the taking and he

could also easily end up dominating that vital open c-file as well.

Dan
According to Dan, the e5-square is just begging to be occupied. Never one to be hanging around, he naturally adopts the good old 'there's no time like the present' adage! Hence the unsurprising 16 ♘e5.

Elizabeth
Elizabeth is also after knight centralisation but has opted for 16 ♘e4 instead. This move performs the dual function of blocking the b7-g2 diagonal and uncovering the c1-rook. On e4 the knight eyes up many interesting squares and supports a possible kingside attack.

| ☐ Anatoly | ☐ Boris | ☐ Chris | ☐ Dan | ☐ Elizabeth |

Points: ....

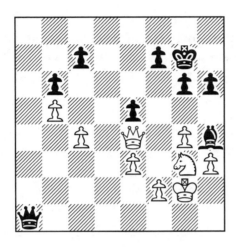

Position after 36...♛a1

White to play

A queen and knight pairing is known as the most deadly attacking force but in the position above you don't exactly see the black king quaking in its boots! Consider whether White should bother preventing Black from trading his bishop for that knight and, with that decision in mind, choose from our panel's selection of moves.

Anatoly

Anatoly obviously thinks that White shouldn't prevent the exchange, advocating 37 ♕c6 in order to get to grips immediately with Black's weak c7-pawn.

Boris

Neither does Boris, who thinks along the same long-term lines as Anatoly but instead prefers 37 ♕d5. He believes that it is important to keep the queen centralised, and if the knight isn't taken on Black's next turn then it will hop into e4.

Chris

Chris does want to keep the knight alive and with 37 ♘f1 he has the manoeuvre ♘d2 (or ♘h2)-f3 in mind.

Dan

Dan dismisses our debate out of hand in view of 37 f4. Clearly he believes that there are other considerations and he has bigger fish to fry!

Elizabeth

Like Chris, Elizabeth does want to preserve her steed and recommends 37 ♘h1 to put the knight on defensive duty.

☐ Anatoly ☐ Boris ☐ Chris ☐ Dan ☐ Elizabeth

Points: ....

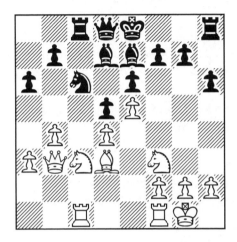

Position after 15 ♕b3

Black to play
Who do you think has the right idea about this position?

Anatoly
Black should play 15...g5, when the kingside initiative should give him the upper hand. Unlike Black, White has already committed his king.

Boris
Black should play 15...b5, when a possible queenside initiative should give him the upper hand. Remember, he has the bishop pair advantage which bodes well for later on.

Chris
Chris believes that whatever Black does, White should have a fairly comfortable edge. He has a space advantage on the queenside (which could aid in a ♘a4-c5 manoeuvre) as well as advanced pawns

in the centre which offer a good springboard for a kingside attack should the black king commit itself there. Black has the two bishops but White has retained his 'good' bishop and doesn't experience any of the cramping that Black does.

Dan
Black should play 15...f5. If this pawn is taken (en passant) then his dark-squared bishop will come to life and White's d-pawn can expect some grief. However, if the pawn remains on f5 then Black can safely castle due to a lack of problems along the b1-h7 diagonal. All in all, Black stands better.

Elizabeth
With all things considered, apparently sitting on the fence, Elizabeth has declared a 'dynamic equilibrium' with chances being equal!

☐ Anatoly ☐ Boris ☐ Chris ☐ Dan ☐ Elizabeth

Points: ....

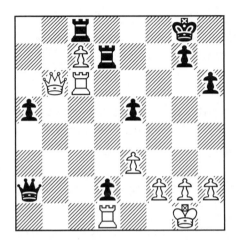

Position after 29...♛xa2

White to play
A crazy position taken from a real-life, top-level encounter. There are pawns close to promotion, rooks that can be attacked and back rank problems for both sides to consider. Get your thinking cap on and then advise White on the best way forward.

Anatoly
Anatoly recommends a time-out for White in the form of 30 g3. This provides some 'luft' for his king and with the inevitable tactics ensures that he won't get mated on the back rank.

Boris
Boris is thinking along the same lines as Anatoly but proposes that in fact 30 h3 is more accurate as his king will be safer on h2.

Chris
Chris is tendering 30 ♖d6 as the best move. The rook gets behind

Black's passed pawn whilst simultaneously challenging Black's rook. Throw in with this the chance to arrange ♖d8+ and you can see its attraction.

Dan
It's straight in for Dan. Often the most obvious move is the best and hence Dan's decision to go for 30 ♛b8.

Elizabeth
Elizabeth agrees with Dan that the rook on c8 needs to be pressurised without delay but for various reasons she considers 30 ♛b7 to be a stronger move.

☐ Anatoly ☐ Boris   ☐ Chris   ☐ Dan   ☐ Elizabeth

Points: ....

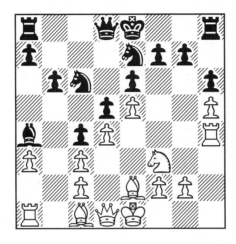

Position after 13 ♗e2

Black to play
White seems to be gearing up for a possible kingside attack. However, it's Black to move. Have you got any advice for him?

Anatoly
Anatoly is advocating the move 13...♔d7 here. As the centre is closed, the monarch will be perfectly safe there and the queen is offered an alternative to the traditional ways of entering the action.

Boris
Boris has a tendency to laugh in the face of danger. It's a controversial decision but he wants to castle kingside now with the aim of utilising his f-pawn to pressurise White's centre. The f-file also seems like the most likely candidate for Black's rooks to find some action.

Chris

Chris sees White's weak queenside pawns as something to target. The bishop is hitting c2 but he has come up with a plan of manoeuvring a knight to b5. For him it is a toss up between 13...a6 and 13...a5, both facilitating ...♘a7.

Dan

Dan wants to get things going on the queenside a bit quicker than that. He is looking to advance his pawns over there and that explains why he wants to whip out 13...b5.

Elizabeth

Elizabeth has listened to the queenside ambitions of Chris and Dan but cannot condone the lack of attention concerning the placing of the king and the major pieces. Instead she wants to keep things nice and simple via 13...♕d7. On her next turn Elizabeth has every intention of castling long.

☐ Anatoly	☐ Boris	☐ Chris	☐ Dan	☐ Elizabeth

Points: ....

Position after 71 ♗xf5

Black to play
It's Black to play in a position taken from an encounter between two of the world's leading players. What should happen?

Anatoly
Anatoly believes that the game is destined to be a draw despite Black's two-pawn material plus. His logic is twofold: firstly, Black's g-pawn will have severe difficulty negotiating g4 due to the important opposite-coloured bishop feature in the position and, secondly, the fact that Black has the wrong bishop for the h-pawn queening square proves decisive.

Boris
Boris disagrees with his fellow countryman's first claim, advocating that 71...g5+ puts Black on a path to victory.

Chris

Chris buys the first part of Anatoly's argument but, regarding the second point, believes that this would only be relevant if the white king could make it back to the corner. After the obvious 71...gxf5, he doesn't believe that it can.

Dan

Dan wants to flick in the move 71...♝g3+, believing that Black can win after the sequence 72 ♔e4 gxf5+.

Elizabeth

Elizabeth also wants to intervene with a check but differs from Dan in that her view is 71...♝g5+ would ultimately secure the full point.

☐ Anatoly ☐ Boris ☐ Chris ☐ Dan ☐ Elizabeth

Points: ....

Now turn to page 127 for the solutions to Test 3

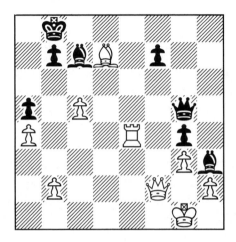

Position after 38...♛g5

White to play
Don't spend too much time on this one because I would like you to put yourselves into White's shoes in the above position. You are nicely up on material but you are very short on time. What should you do?

Anatoly
Anatoly recommends centralising the queen in order to keep a firm grip on the position. Hence his decision to select 39 ♕f5 as White's next move.

Boris
Due to the black bishop on h3, the white king is a little on the ropes. 39 ♕xf7 bags a pawn and offers the king f2 as a flight square.

Chris

Chris thinks that White's own king is fairly safe where it stands. He is advocating 39 c6 in order to start to expose the enemy monarch. He has spotted the tactic 39...♗b6 but believes that he can more than adequately deal with that via 40 c7+.

Dan

Dan is thinking along the same lines as Chris but instead is looking to land the sequence 39 c6 ♗b6 40 ♖e8+. That will see him through to the 40-move time control with a completely winning position.

Elizabeth

It's at times like this that Elizabeth advises against doing anything too radical. She suggests keeping a lid on the position, considering both 39 ♗f5 and 39 ♕e3 to be safe moves. For the time being either of those would do her fine.

☐ Anatoly ☐ Boris ☐ Chris ☐ Dan ☐ Elizabeth

Points: ....

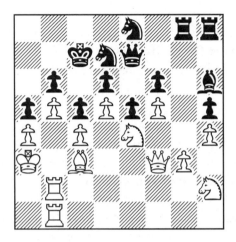

Position after 61...♕e7

White to play
White has a very comfortable space advantage, but in a fairly closed position is there any way for him to break through?

Anatoly
Yes, and now is the time to strike whilst the iron is hot according to Anatoly. Whilst Black's pieces languish on the kingside he wants to crash through on the queenside. After 62 ♗xa5, if 62...bxa5 then 63 b6+ donates the b5-square to White as a means to infiltrate Black's position.

Boris
Boris wants to mix things up in a different way. He likes the idea of grabbing a pawn. Okay, after 62 ♕xh5 ♗c1 it is essentially an exchange sacrifice, but White will then have plenty of time to advance his kingside pawn majority.

Chris

Chris wants to create some action on the g-file. Kicking off with 62 ♖g2, his intention is to double rooks and then to break with g3-g4.

Dan

Dan is thinking along similar lines to Chris but believes that the immediate 62 g4 is the right course of action. By playing it now, the opponent will have no time to coordinate his forces.

Elizabeth

Although most would prefer White's position, Elizabeth has a word of warning. She has often seen this sort of position go pear shaped. Whilst she acknowledges that g3-g4 is the only realistic break for White, her opinion is that the decision to effectively saddle one-self with an isolated pawn could see the tables being turned. Her expected sequence would be 62 ♔a2 ♘g7 (to protect the h-pawn) with a draw in the not too distant future a reasonable result for both sides.

☐ Anatoly ☐ Boris ☐ Chris ☐ Dan ☐ Elizabeth

Points: ....

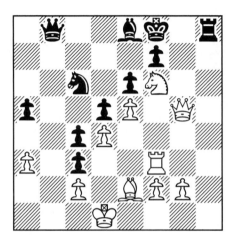

Position after 27...bxc3

White to play
Can you advise White in this potentially tactical middlegame?

Anatoly
'Niet!' exclaims Anatoly, who doesn't want to have anything to do with White's position. According to him, White has clearly over-pressed and is about to be on the end of a serious backlash.

Boris
Boris isn't quite so negative. He believes that White must hang on to his d-pawn, though, and hence his suggestion of 28 ♖f4.

Chris
Chris recommends seeking a trade of rooks via 28 ♖h3. This both minimises Black's counterplay and removes a key defender.

Dan

Dan suggests that White must grab this opportunity to engage in a spot of sacrificing. His opinion is that 28 ♘d7+ is White's best move here, and without this he is probably worse.

Elizabeth

Elizabeth wants to remain composed. The simple 28 ♖xc3 removes the most dangerous of Black's threats and leaves White very slightly better.

☐ Anatoly ☐ Boris   ☐ Chris   ☐ Dan   ☐ Elizabeth

Points: ....

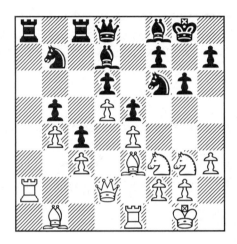

Position after 23...♛d8

White to play
Regarding the candidate moves for White in the above position, can you sort the wheat from the chaff in order to determine your preferred continuation?

Anatoly
It's an odd-looking move, but Anatoly likes 24 ♗a7 with the main purpose of avoiding rook trades on the a-file.

Boris
Boris suggests 24 ♗h6. Following the inevitable trade of bishops, he intends to set about exploiting the holes in Black's defensive shell.

Chris
Chris feels that this position has obviously arisen from a Ruy Lopez and in this position the manoeuvre ♘h2-g4 frequently comes into

play. He knows that he will require more control over the g4-square but for now is quite happy with 24 ♘h2.

Dan
Dan wants to get to grips with the pawn on g6 and is thus turning to the standard h-pawn advance. Yes, it's 24 h4, intending h4-h5 next turn. Dan wants to give Black something to think about on the king-side.

Elizabeth
Elizabeth believes that there are several sensible moves for White here but with little to choose between them she has opted for 24 ♗g5. It's a simple pin which is slightly awkward for Black to escape and though hardly a radical move, it is a step in the right direction.

☐ Anatoly	☐ Boris	☐ Chris	☐ Dan	☐ Elizabeth

Points: ....

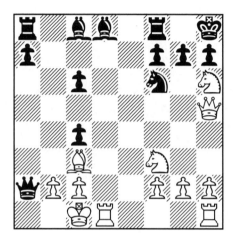

Position after 18...♘f6

White to play
Time for a tactical excerpt from a famous encounter. Beware that all may not be as it seems and, with that in mind, uncover the best move in this position.

Anatoly
Despite the threat to his own king, Anatoly believes that White should not be worse after the visual 19 ♘g5.

Boris
19 ♖xd8 is Boris's poison, with ♘xf7+ up next.

Chris
Chris is showing a bit of creativity here and has taken a shine to 19 ♕xf7, when back rank tricks and smothered mates abound.

Dan

As far as Dan is concerned White must buy some time for the queen. Hence his decision to kick off with 19 ♗xf6. Upon 19...♗xf6 he intends 20 ♘xf7+, very grateful that his king has a valid escape route via d2.

Elizabeth

It's no frills for Elizabeth. From experience she knows that one should always look out for checks and she believes that the most accurate continuation is the straightforward 19 ♘xf7+.

☐ Anatoly ☐ Boris   ☐ Chris   ☐ Dan   ☐ Elizabeth

Points: ....

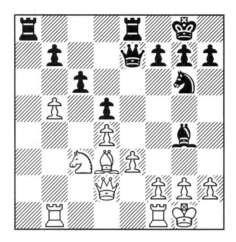

Position after 18 ♕xd2

Black to play
White's good old queenside 'minority attack' is clearly very much under way. Which of our panel do you believe understands the correct way to react to this standard positional plan?

Anatoly
Black must act quickly on the kingside according to Anatoly, who recommends deploying the h-pawn. The idea behind 18...h5 is, if allowed, to advance this pawn all the way to h3. The intention is to weaken White's defensive shell and, put bluntly, ultimately aim for a mate on g2.

Boris
Boris also believes that Black should concentrate his efforts on the kingside but differs from Anatoly in that he prefers a piece attack. For him Black should kick off with 18...♘h4 because it creates all sorts of tactical threats around g2 and f3.

Chris

Chris feels that Black shouldn't be putting all of his eggs into one basket just yet. He thinks that 18...♗d7 should hold the queenside together, particularly after 19 bxc6 ♗xc6. With ...f7-f5 also in the reckoning should White not trade on c6, Black will have plenty of time to go after the white monarch.

Dan

Dan is eager to have more of a say in the centre. Ironically he hints that a premature kingside offensive 'smacks of desperation' and personally prefers to play for ...c6-c5. Besides, his logic is 'how can a centralising rook move be wrong?' and hence his decision to plump for the d5-supporting 18...♖ad8.

Elizabeth

Elizabeth wants to see White's queenside exertions backfire. The a-file has been opened and she wants to put it to good use. Essentially she hopes to start an invasion of her own and thus offers up the rook-doubling preparation 18...♖a3.

☐ Anatoly	☐ Boris	☐ Chris	☐ Dan	☐ Elizabeth
Points:				

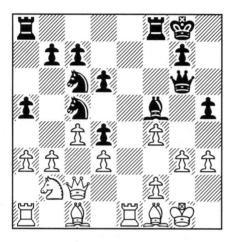

Position after 18 ♗f1

Black to play
Although White has the bishop pair in the above position, the fact
that he has no pieces beyond the second rank clearly offers Black
some reasonable compensation for his pawn deficit. Which move
most justifies Black's situation?

Anatoly
There is an open file that must be challenged according to Anatoly
who, opting not to calculate too much here, insists on 18...♖ae8. His
only debate was which rook to switch and he feels that in these
circumstances one is temporarily best left on the f-file.

Boris
Boris suggests that as most of White's pieces are languishing on
the queenside, the time is right for a kingside attack. With that in
mind he has little hesitation in suggesting 18...h4.

Chris

Chris feels that a good plan should involve exploiting the poor placing of the b2-knight. He proposes 18...♖ab8 with the intention being to launch his own b-pawn to b5. Fairly transparently, Black intends hunting White's b-pawn and believes that his opponent will suffer due to a lack of piece coordination through a lack of space.

Dan

Dan agrees with Chris that the key to quick activity involves the pressurising of White's b-pawn but instead offers up 18...♖a6. The intention is to manoeuvre the rook to b6 in order to highlight White's lack of defenders for b3.

Elizabeth

Not just the pawn, but the square b3 is what Elizabeth is after. She has taken a fancy to the advance 18...a4 as after the expected response 19 b4 she very much likes the idea of parking her knight on the newly created outpost. Fundamental to her concept is the weakness that is White's d3-pawn - it is a target very much in her sights.

☐ Anatoly ☐ Boris ☐ Chris ☐ Dan ☐ Elizabeth

Points: ....

Test Four

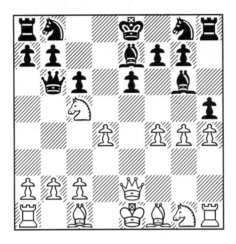

Position after 9...h5

White to play
Black has just played 9...h5. This pressurises White's g-pawn and as well as creating a safe haven for his bishop, also looks to gain access to the f5-square. How should White best respond?

Anatoly
Anatoly has thought long and hard about the position and has decided that 10 g5 must be best. Although this may be playing into Black's hands regarding the f5-square, it at least removes possibilities from the g8-knight. Furthermore, the variation 10...♗xc5 11 dxc5 ♕xc5 is now a reasonable positional pawn sacrifice due to the weakened dark squares in the black camp.

Boris
Boris can see no suitable alternative to the straightforward 10 gxh5. This does concede the f5-square but rather than allowing Black to capture on g4 on his own terms, it has the advantage of

giving Black a difficult decision to have to make.

Chris
It appears that for the time being at least, Chris is happy to ignore the kingside tension. Indeed, with his recommendation of 10 ♖h3 he intends swinging the rook into action via b3. This exploits the exposed nature of the black queen and actively seeks to zap the b7-pawn.

Dan
It's a case of 'all or nothing' for Dan, who wants to crash through with 10 ♘xe6. His justification, backed up by a certain amount of analysis, is that Black's pieces are offside. White's own queen will prove to be the bane of Black's position and the rest of the white army can soon surge through the centre.

Elizabeth
Elizabeth advocates a different positional pawn sacrifice. After 10 f5 exf5 11 g5, not only will Black be deprived the use of the f5-square, but then White will have access to f4 for her own purposes.

☐ Anatoly	☐ Boris	☐ Chris	☐ Dan	☐ Elizabeth
Points:				

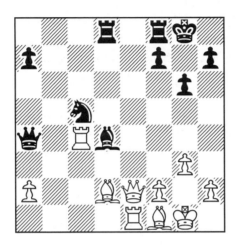

Position after 22 ♖c4

Black to play

White has two bishops in an open position but that is not Black's only worry. His centrally posted pieces are a tad precariously placed and of course his queen is currently attacked. I wouldn't be surprised if you would rather not have anything to do with this sticky situation. However, your mission (should you choose to accept it!) is to select the best practical path available to Black.

Anatoly

According to Anatoly there are no tactical variations that will save Black here and so he has fallen back on the solid queen centralisation 22...♕d7. At least with this move everything remains protected.

Boris

For Boris the black queen is better off along the h1-a8 diagonal and thus his liking of 22...♕c6. Clearly he prefers adding extra support to the knight rather than the bishop.

Chris
Chris believes that he has found the solution to most of Black's problems in 22...♖fe8. He will still have some work to do to hold the ensuing two bishops versus bishop and knight situation but thanks to Black's better placed pieces, the prospects for a draw are good.

Dan
Dan's radically different view is that it is White that will be grateful for the draw after 22...♗xf2+. Only a temporary piece sacrifice, after the forced 23 ♔xf2 ♕xa2 it is White who will feel the pinch.

Elizabeth
Effectively, Elizabeth's opinion is that Black is destined to lose the exchange. With this in mind she favours 22...♕xa2 to at least put something in the bank.

☐ Anatoly ☐ Boris   ☐ Chris   ☐ Dan   ☐ Elizabeth

Points: ....

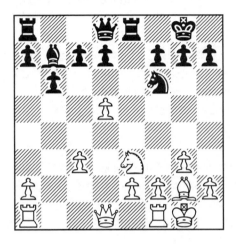

Position after 15 bxc3

Black to play
Who do you think has the best move and accompanying justification in the above position?

Anatoly
Anatoly believes that Black should play 15...d6 here. This fixes White's pawn on a light square and provides Black's remaining two minor pieces with extra options. The bishop could always spring to action via the c8-h3 diagonal, whilst the knight is granted access to the d7-square from which it could hop to either e5 or c5.

Boris
Boris wants to get straight to the nitty-gritty of the position. Although he acknowledges that 15...♛e7 would be a useful move, here it falls foul of 16 d6!. Hence he doesn't want to beat about the bush and tenders 15...h5. With the idea of advancing this pawn further, he clearly fancies teasing White's kingside weaknesses.

Chris

Chris feels that this position offers a perfect opportunity for one of those fancy exchange sacrifices. After 15...♖xe3 16 fxe3 d6 the positional compensation is then more than adequate.

Dan

Dan is desperate (yet again!) to get to grips with White's pawn centre and believes 15...c6 to be thematic. Currently White has a space advantage and more centralisation, but according to Dan Black's superior pawn structure counterbalances the situation.

Elizabeth

In a very elegant manner (naturally!), Elizabeth wants to pick up her knight and drop it on to the attractive e4-square. She feels it is important that Black plays this now before White can centralise the queen. With ...♕f6 in the air, she is also happy with the sequence 15...♘e4 16 ♕d4 c5.

□ Anatoly □ Boris	□ Chris	□ Dan	□ Elizabeth
Points:			

Now turn to page 137 for the solutions to Test 4

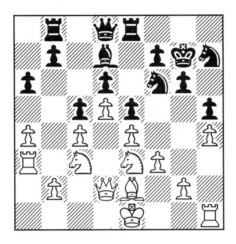

Position after 18...♕d8

White to play
White has a space advantage in the above position, but which plan do you believe is the most likely to turn the heat up on the opponent?

Anatoly
According to Anatoly White should concentrate his efforts on the queenside. He should kick off with 19 a5 to gain a firm grip on the b6-square. It should then be his aim to occupy that very square with a knight with a ♘c3-a4-b6 manoeuvre, closely followed up by a b2-b4 pawn break. To free up the h1-rook for queenside action, he believes that the white monarch should set up home on f2.

Boris
Boris also believes that the queenside is where it's at, at least until Black blocks things up with ...a6-a5 (thus eliminating his own chance of counterplay). He advocates 19 0-0 with the intention of ♖b1 to

support the b4 break. He disagrees with Anatoly in the concept of a4-a5. If Black advances his own a-pawn only then will the kingside avenue be explored; White then has all the time in the world.

Chris
Chris believes that White should be focusing on the kingside and given the current h-pawn situation, suggests that 19 g4 rather jumps out as more than just a candidate! Ultimately of course the aim is to create a serious attack down the h-file, although Chris acknowledges that some persuasion may be required to provoke ...hxg4. He has in mind a manoeuvre of a knight to g3 with the other steed probably setting up a base on f2 in order to protect e4 and support g4.

Dan
It is Dan's opinion that the most fruitful pawn break is going to be f3-f4 and he can't wait to get his major pieces employed along that file. He proposes 19 0-0 with 20 f4 up next. Ideally he would like to swing the a3-rook along to f3 but recognises that the piece congestion along the third rank makes that a little difficult. Hence after probably making the recapture ♖xf4 (assuming Black trades pawns), he will adopt the manoeuvre ♖a3-a1-f1 for a spot of doubling up.

Elizabeth
Elizabeth supports Dan's policy of f4 but would in general prefer to be recapturing with a pawn in order to build up a big centre. Hence she favours 19 g3 but accepts that more preparatory moves may be required in order to achieve her desired break. The likes of ♗d3, ♕g2, ♔d2-c2 and even ♖a3-a1 are all possibly on her agenda before the big breakthrough occurs. Essentially, with Black's potential counterplay under control, she will happily take her time.

☐ Anatoly	☐ Boris	☐ Chris	☐ Dan	☐ Elizabeth

Points: ....

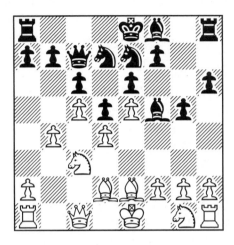

Position after 11...g5

White to play
Black has just played the bold 11...g5. Should White pinpoint this as
a weakness in constructing a middlegame plan?

Anatoly
'Definitely' is Anatoly's opinion, and so keen is he to highlight this
fact, he wants to whip out 12 g4. His idea is to fix the pawn on g5
and then challenge it with h2-h4. The likelihood is that White will
win a pawn on the kingside.

Boris
Boris also wants to exploit the g5-pawn but prefers to go down the
direct route. He favours the immediate 12 h4. His expectation is
that Black will respond with 12...g4 and then the thematic 13 h5 for
all intents and purposes isolates the pawn on g4.

Chris

Chris agrees that the pawn on g5 is a weakness and that its advance has created holes around it. However, he doesn't believe that this factor should alter his main plan of expansion on the queenside. For him it was a toss up between 12 a4 and 12 b5 and he has gone with the latter simply because 12...cxb5 is unplayable anyway.

Dan

Dan is adamant that the cheeky 11...g5 was premature and he wants to use this to his advantage immediately. Destined to castle kingside, he views the f-file as his future and hence his decision to plump for 12 f4.

Elizabeth

It appears that all of our panel are critical of 11...g5 although Elizabeth can see no justification for radical chess. It is no great surprise, then, that she is more than happy with the straightforward 12 ♘f3, simply preparing to castle kingside. Elizabeth believes that the time will come to turn up the heat but for now simple development should be the order of the day.

☐ Anatoly	☐ Boris	☐ Chris	☐ Dan	☐ Elizabeth
Points:				

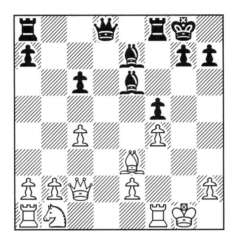

Position after 17 gxf4

Black to play
In the fairly open position above, Black has the bishop pair to compensate him for his pawn deficit. Which plan do you believe is most likely to provide something substantial?

Anatoly
Anatoly believes that Black should concentrate most of his efforts on the kingside. Although White could put the half-open g-file to good use given time, he advocates anticipating this via 17...h6. Before White can arrange ♔h1 and ♖g1, Black's g-pawn will have a positive role to play with ...g5.

Boris
Boris also wants his g-pawn involved but somewhat sooner. Indeed, the immediate 17...g5 rings his chimes. Although he concedes that Black could emerge with four isolated pawns, his opinion is that it will be White who will suffer from the opening of the g-file.

Chris

Chris similarly believes that the g-file as well as the h-file is critical as Black should engage in a kingside offensive. He has taken a shine to the rook lift 17...♖f6 and fully intends to support it with a bishop along the b7-g2 diagonal and the queen via e8.

Dan

Taking a completely different stance, Dan is eager to put the half-open b-file to good use. Kicking off with 17...♗f6, he plans to continue with ...♕a5 and ...♖b8. The order in which these two moves would most likely appear depends on how White responds, but his short-term aim is clearly to pressurise b2 and in the long term the whole of White's queenside.

Elizabeth

Elizabeth admits that both the g-file and the b-file have their attractions but nevertheless she likes the sly move 17...♖e8. Yes, she has uncovered a third option in the form of the half-open e-file. Currently a white bishop rests there unprotected and her main middlegame strategy revolves around pressurising the pawn on e2.

□ Anatoly □ Boris □ Chris □ Dan □ Elizabeth

Points: ....

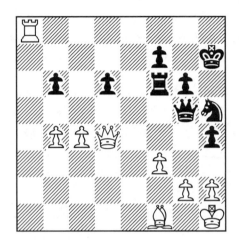

Position after 36 ♖a8

Black to play

It's time for a tactical episode from a recent real-life encounter. In the above position, what is the story about the sacrifice 36...♘g3+ here? Remember, do all the calculations in your head, i.e. if you set the position up on a board, don't move the pieces!

Anatoly

Anatoly believes that he has analysed all of the variations and his conclusion is that it is a very strong move and that Black is at least slightly better in all lines.

Boris

Boris believes that the move is only successful if White accepts the piece offering. Upon 37 ♔g1 White is at least equal.

Chris

Chris thinks that White should accept the offering but will be able to avoid defeat by utilising a later ♖h8+ counter-sacrifice in order to obtain a perpetual check.

Dan
Dan believes that 36...♘g3+ is desperation and that after 37 hxg3 White can defend against an h-file assault with a timely ♗e2.

Elizabeth
Elizabeth is advocating the defence 37 hxg3 hxg3 38 ♗d3, when after 38...♕h6+ 39 ♔g1 ♕h2+ 40 ♔f1 the white king can do a runner. Her conclusion is that White is most certainly not worse.

☐ Anatoly ☐ Boris ☐ Chris ☐ Dan ☐ Elizabeth

Points: ....

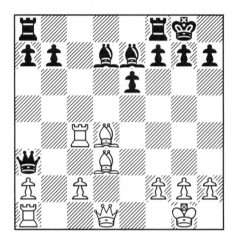

Position after 17...♕a3

White to play
On the way to the above position Black has pinched a hot pawn and White is now considering how to exact punishment. Should White be tempted by a sacrifice?

Anatoly
Anatoly thinks so although it's only a temporary one. After 18 ♗xg7 ♔xg7 19 ♕g4+, because of the check on d4 White will re-establish material equilibrium but with positional features (e.g. the exposed nature of the black king) then favouring him.

Boris
Certainly according to Boris, who has confidently declared 18 ♗xh7+ to be a forced win.

Chris
Chris doesn't think that the time is right just yet particularly with

18 ♗e4 available. Okay, the bishop would pressurise Black's queen-side but more to the point the path is cleared for ♖c3 followed by a bishop sacrifice and rook swinger to the kingside sequence. Twinning that with ♕h5 and the future looks bleak for Black!

Dan
It seems that Dan is slowly maturing even throughout the course of this book because rather than barging in like a bull in a china shop he is advocating 18 ♕g4. Basically, though, he is desperate for mate and views g7 as the best target.

Elizabeth
Elizabeth also wants to preserve her bishops for the time being and believes that White's task is actually quite simple. She wants to kick off with 18 ♕h5, citing the variation 18...g6 19 ♕h6 f6 20 ♗xg6 as an example of why patience is a virtue.

☐ Anatoly ☐ Boris   ☐ Chris   ☐ Dan   ☐ Elizabeth

Points: ....

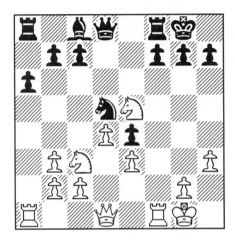

Position after 13...♘d5

White to play
White has a well placed knight on e5 and a handy half-open file in the above position. How should he put these features to good use?

Anatoly
There is hardly a more direct route than that suggested by our Russian contingent. According to Anatoly, 14 ♖xf7 should lead to a favourable endgame.

Boris
Boris instead suggests the tactical recipe 14 ♘xf7. By the way, he is not especially looking for an endgame!

Chris
Chris's plan involves the doubling or even trebling of the major pieces on the f-file. Simple chess rather than creation according to Chris is 14 ♘xd5 ♕xd5 15 ♖f4 with the advance c2-c4 available to

White whenever he wants it.

Dan

Dan wants to get the heavy artillery in on the attack. In the quest to further pressurise f7 he rates 14 ♕h5. As well as having to worry about his king, Black must beware the potential danger to his (or her) d5-knight.

Elizabeth

Smooth as you like, Elizabeth is attracted to the idea of 14 ♘xe4. Although 14...♘xe3 15 ♕h5 is indeed an exchange sacrifice, her logic is that the queen and two knights (as well as one rook on the f-file) will overwhelm the enemy monarch.

☐ Anatoly ☐ Boris ☐ Chris ☐ Dan ☐ Elizabeth

Points: ....

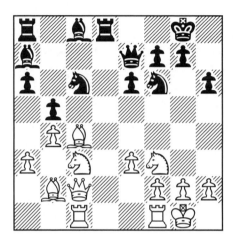

Position after 14...b5

White to play
You're going to hate me for this one, no doubt tendering those arguments about 'a matter of taste' etc etc! Anyway, Black has just
attacked White's light-squared bishop. Who in your opinion has the
most applicable plan to deal with this situation?

Anatoly
Anatoly has foreseen that White can generate a very reasonable
kingside attack if he starts with 14 ♗a2. This is a standard retreat
that prepares 15 ♗b1. With the queen and bishop aligned on this
important diagonal, Black will suffer much anxiety regarding tactics
involving a future ♕h7+. Note that although deceptively distant,
the b2-bishop will have a big say in the middlegame too.

Boris
Boris wants to strike while the iron is hot. Rather than deliberating
about where the bishop should retreat to, he wants to grab two

pawns for it here and now. After 14 ♗xb5 axb5 15 ♘xb5 White will have a pair of dangerous connected passed pawns and plenty of pieces to help support their advance.

Chris

Chris has come up with a plan that kicks off with 14 ♗d3. Next on White's agenda will be 15 ♘e4 and the result will be some fantastically open lines for White's bishops. Despite apparently having to make a decision now as to which side of the board to show its allegiance to, in fact the light-squared bishop could soon find itself having a big influence on both sides of the board.

Dan

Not renowned for his patience, Dan has jumped in all guns blazing with 14 ♘xb5. He's keeping tight-lipped about this one!

Elizabeth

Elizabeth sees Black's pawn on b5 as a weakness and recommends sliding the bishop back to e2. It doesn't get in the way of the d-file there and, whilst eyeing up b5 now, could later change diagonals by transferring to f3.

☐ Anatoly	☐ Boris	☐ Chris	☐ Dan	☐ Elizabeth

Points: ....

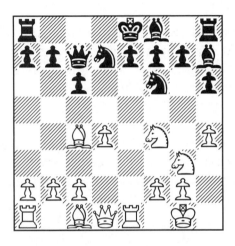

Position after 11 ♖e1

Black to play
It is Black to play in the above position. What move/plan is the best solution to the problems that he is experiencing with his f-pawn and the e-file?

Anatoly
A standard Caro Kann manoeuvre 11...♘b6, intending 12 ♗b3 ♘bd5, shores up the centre according to Anatoly, who believes that it is important to lock out White's light-squared bishop.

Boris
Boris can't see Black making a challenge of this position until he completes his development. Hence his automatic selection of 11...e6, bolstering the d5-square and freeing the dark-squared bishop.

Chris
Chris has come up with the amazing 11...♗g8. The idea he explains is

to have the bishop support both f7 and e6 (for when he advances this e-pawn). He acknowledges that the bishop looks daft here but will return it to more active duty once the coast is clear.

Dan

Dan has been itching to get castled with 11...0-0-0. Though apparently ignoring White's threats, with the kings on opposite sides of the board, the intention is to make White suffer for having advanced a vital pawn around his king.

Elizabeth

Thinking along similar lines to Dan, Elizabeth fancies 11...g5 only because her own monarch hasn't been committed to that side of the board. Pushing away the knight from f4 will relieve much of the pressure that White is currently exerting.

☐ Anatoly ☐ Boris   ☐ Chris   ☐ Dan   ☐ Elizabeth

Points: ....

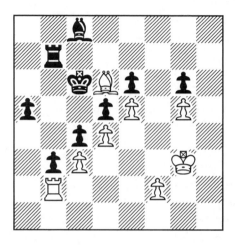

Position after 50 &g3

Black to play
Who in your opinion holds the most realistic view regarding Black's
winning chances or lack of in the above ending?

Anatoly
Although Black has two extra connected queenside pawns, the opposite-coloured bishops unfortunately (i.e. for the second player)
extremely limit the prospects of a win. The main stumbling block
according to Anatoly is the lack of entry points into the enemy position. Certainly there is no way in for the black king or bishop,
whilst White's pieces can just about keep the black rook out of serious action.

Boris
Boris disagrees, with the key factor in his opinion being the available infiltration of the black rook via the h-file.

Chris

Like Boris, Chris believes that an invasion with the black rook will certainly guarantee victory, although he only believes that this is possible via the a-file. His recommendation is 50...a4 with the intention being to jettison this pawn to White's bishop on a3 in order to gain access.

Dan

A pattern is forming as Dan agrees with Chris that it is all about the a-file. He wants to keep his a-pawn though and suggests the manoeuvre ...♖b4-a4 as being very promising.

Elizabeth

Elizabeth has a completely different view about how Black should set about winning this position. Her logic is that Black wants to get in ...a4-a3 and so the removal of White's bishop is a practical necessity. She is prepared to sacrifice her rook for it. Though this is not an easy task she nevertheless believes it is possible to force such a trade if the appropriate king and rook placement is adopted.

☐ Anatoly ☐ Boris   ☐ Chris   ☐ Dan   ☐ Elizabeth

Points: ....

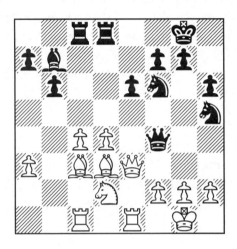

Position after 22 &c3

Black to play
White has the bishop pair but in the above position it is his opponent who has the superior pawn structure. Can you suggest a suitable idea for Black in this fascinating middlegame?

Anatoly
Anatoly recommends getting to grips with White's weaknesses. He
has pinpointed the hanging pawns as natural targets and, as a toss
up between 22...&d7 and 22...&c7, has opted for the flexibility of
the latter to facilitate the doubling of rooks on either the c-file or
the d-file.

Boris
Boris wants to take advantage of the loose bishop on d3 and has
spotted the interesting tactic 22...e5. This really puts the question
to the white centre and, whilst threatening to isolate White's c-
pawn, one should note that his intention is to meet 23 d5 with

23...♗xd5.

Chris
In Chris's opinion Black should prefer preserving the queens. More to the point, the h5-knight could do with seeing some more action. Through 22...♕b8 two birds are killed with one stone. Whilst the intriguing possibility of 23...♕a8 becomes available, possibly of more relevance is that the f4-square has been vacated for occupation by a black steed.

Dan
Is it desperation or is it pure genius? Dan has come up with 22...♗xg2 and, intending 23 ♔xg2 ♘g4, believes that the forking abilities of the two knights help provide adequate compensation for any material sacrificed in the ensuing variations.

Elizabeth
Like most of our panel, Elizabeth believes that Black should be focusing on getting a knight to f4. Via 22...♘g4, also bringing the f6-steed into action, this aim will be achieved. She doesn't particularly object to having the queens traded on her terms because the more exchanges there are, the weaker she feels White's hanging pawns will become.

☐ Anatoly   ☐ Boris   ☐ Chris   ☐ Dan   ☐ Elizabeth

Points: ....

Now turn to page 149 for the solutions to Test 5

Solutions To Test One

Solution 1-1

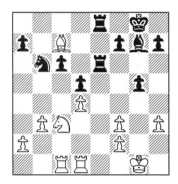

There were five very plausible answers although I don't buy Anatoly's analysis - it must be sensible to keep control of the only open file on the board.

It's always worth trying to improve the placing of pieces that aren't pulling their weight and here that particularly applies to the king and knight. I am going to award points for the other answers but I believe that my decision is justified by the following:

Seger-Sadler
Bundesliga 2003
22...♘c8! 23 ♔f1 ♘e7 24 ♖c2 ♘f5

A peach of a square!

25 ♘e2 ♖h6 26 ♗g3 ♖xh3 27 ♖d3 ♖h1+ 28 ♔g2 ♖e1 29 ♖dd2 h5 30 ♔h3 ♔h7 31 ♔h2 ♖e6 32 ♗b8 ♘h4 33 ♔g3 ♖6xe2 0-1

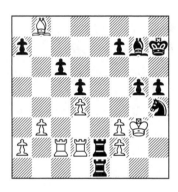

The point is 34 ♖xe2 ♖g1+ 35 ♔h3 ♘xf3 and, following a superb demonstration of utilising simple chess to exploit weaknesses, mate is forthcoming.

Points
Anatoly 2
Boris 4
Chris 10
Dan 3
Elizabeth 5

Solution 1-2
(see following diagram)
I'm not keen on Dan's idea at all.

Although there is a black pawn fixed on e5, the dark-squared bishop would still have plenty of scope after a bishop-for-knight trade by White. Indeed after, say, 24 ♗c5 ♕b7 25 ♖xd8+ ♖xd8 26 ♗xb4 axb4 27 ♘e2 ♗g5 Black would have plenty of activity. Besides, the intermezzo 26...♖d4!? may simply be quite powerful. Note that strong players are often cautious about conceding bishops for knights.

and making way for the re-introduction of the white knight. Its enemy number has a less promising future.

27...♖f8 28 ♘d2 ♗d8 29 ♘f3 f6 30 ♖d2 ♗e7 31 ♕e6!

The invasion begins!

31...♖ad8 32 ♖xd8! ♗xd8

Upon 32...♖xd8 White has the crushing 33 ♘xe5!, for example 33...fxe5 34 ♖f7+.

33 ♖d1 ♘b8 34 ♗c5 ♖h8

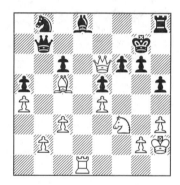

The other suggestions are very reasonable, as would be something involving ♘e2. Maximum points, though, must go to Anatoly and how fitting that we are following the game below.

Karpov-Spassky
Leningrad 1974
24 ♘b1! ♕b7 25 ♔h2!

A precautionary move. There is no need to hurry.

25...♔g7 26 c3 ♘a6 27 ♖e2!

Preserving pieces (frequently advisable when one has a space advantage or a generally freer position)

35 ♖xd8 1-0

Yes, 35 ♖xd8 is decisive in view of 35...♖xd8 36 ♗e7, when the black king is defenceless. As a junior I was a great admirer of Anatoly Karpov and his technique here is impeccable.

Though far from stupid, the plan of Boris (not the real Boris in the above game) isn't too inspirational because too many trades (all of the rooks are destined to be chopped off on the d-line) may steer the game towards a draw. A little credit (but not as much!) goes to Chris and Elizabeth.

Points

Anatoly 10

Boris 4

Chris 5

Dan 1

Elizabeth 5

Solution 1-3

Actually I thought that this one was pretty easy and hence I'm not exactly over-generous with the marking! 34 ♘e3 may run into a tactic involving ...♘xg3 and 34 ♖b1 cxb5 doesn't lead to much. A little analysis, however, should have confirmed that White can't be worse, and indeed Dan is spot on as the following game demonstrates:

Fedorov-Radulski

European Championship,

Batumi 2002

34 c5!

Less visual, but ultimately no less powerful, is 34 bxc6 ♖d6 35 ♖d1 ♖xc6 36 ♖d7 ♖xc4 37 ♖xa7 ♖a4 38 ♘e3. Black's knight on the rim is of no use.

34...bxc5

Or else 35 cxb6 anyway.

35 b6! axb6 36 a7 ♖d8

The only way to halt the promotion.

37 ♖d1!

A deflection that suddenly creates a mirror image of the starting position, when it appeared that Black was the active one.

37...♖a8 38 ♖d7

Now the threat of ♖b7-b8 forces Black to concede serious material.

38...♘g7 39 ♖b7 ♘e8 40 ♖b8 ♖xa7 41 ♖xe8+ ♔f7 42 ♖c8 ♖a3 43 c4 b5 44 ♖c7+ 1-0

Points

Anatoly 0

Boris 0

Chris 0

Dan 10

Elizabeth 2

Solution 1-4

(see following diagram)

Our panel makes some very pertinent points. Black does have the bishop pair but the f3-pawn is a good shield against the b7-g2 diagonal. It does make sense for White to try and trade off one of the bishops as it is generally fair to say that two bishops versus a bishop and knight is more of an advantage than just one bishop versus one knight. Furthermore, the trades will expose Black's isolated pawns as bigger weaknesses and hence the attraction of Boris's plan. Observe the following game:

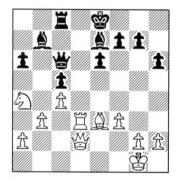

Hector-Timman
Malmö 2003
24 ♗f4! ♗f8

Black may well have seen what was coming but there is nothing that he can do about it. Note that after 24...♖d8 25 ♖xd8+ ♗xd8 26 ♗e3 ♗e7 27 ♕f2 the c5-pawn drops next move.

25 h4

This kingside expansion isn't necessary but it nevertheless demonstrates Black's helplessness.

25...♗e7 26 h5 f6?!

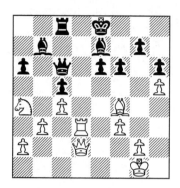

Black would love to get in ...e6-e5 but this only creates an extra weakness on e6.

27 ♗d6 e5 28 ♘xc5! ♗xd6 29 ♘xb7 ♗e7 30 ♘d6+ ♗xd6 31 ♖xd6 ♕b7 32 ♕a5! ♕a7+ 33 ♕b6 1-0

The rook ending holds no hope for Black.

A queenside pawn majority is much more often than not a useful thing in the ending. However, with reference to Dan's plan it seems a shame to trade off Black's c5-pawn when the main game above shows how White could win it free of charge, a task clearly worthy of the white steed's attention.

Points

Anatoly 1
Boris 10
Chris 3
Dan 2
Elizabeth 3

Solution 1-5

I'm not too impressed with Dan's 20 &xa6??, walking into a self-pin. In view of 20...&c6 those who selected this move can count themselves lucky that I'm not deducting points!

Sorry Chris, but although such an idea may be good in another position (for example, when there is a white knight to benefit from the d4- and e5-squares), here 20 b4 cxb4 21 &xc8 bxa3 22 &xf8+ &xf8 just doesn't cut it I'm afraid.

My favourite book as a junior was *Fischer-Spassky Move by Move* and Bobby's choice cuts straight to the chase.

Fischer-Spassky
World Championship (Game 6),
Reykjavik 1972
20 e4! d4?!

Donating to White the square that he was after. Nevertheless, 20...&f6 21 exd5 exd5 22 &f3 would leave White with all the pluses including the chance to ter-

rorise those hanging pawns.
21 f4 &e7 22 e5

White has secured the c4-square for his bishop and the text sees the dark-squared pawns covering more ground and complementing the bishop.
22...&b8 23 &c4 &h8 24 &h3 &f8 25 b3 a5 26 f5 exf5 27 &xf5 &h7 28 &cf1 &d8 29 &g3 &e7 30 h4 &bb7 31 e6! &bc7 32 &e5 &e8 33 a4 &d8 34 &1f2 &e8 35 &2f3 &d8 36 &d3 &e8 37 &e4

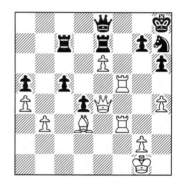

37...&f6

Observe 37...&xe6 38 &f8+ &xf8 39 &xf8+ &xf8 40 &h7 mate.
38 &xf6 gxf6 39 &xf6 &g8 40 &c4 &h8 41 &f4 1-0

Points
Anatoly 3
Boris 10
Chris 1
Dan 0
Elizabeth 4

Solution 1-6

I cannot condone 18 ♗xf6 just because this bishop may soon be temporarily inconvenienced. Black has another knight to replace the one on f6 and both of White's bishops (especially the good dark-squared one) should think of the future.

Without a doubt the most natural plan is to shove the a-pawn up the board and that's why I'm going to award points to both Boris and Elizabeth. However, after 18 a4 a5 it's not that easy to get at the weakened b6-point. Although the b5-square would become an outpost (possibly a long-term home for White's knight), White's light-squared bishop might not be so optimistic.

Anatoly deserves a little credit, although his plan is not very practical and Black's king is after all on the queenside.

After you play over the enlightening game below you will understand why top marks go to Chris.

Korchnoi-Pira
Leipzig 2002
18 ♕b1!

The '!' is not just for this move, but for the ensuing plan too.
18...♘h5 19 ♗d1 g6 20 ♗a4

And this is why White didn't want his pawn on a4. Very instructive!
20...f6 21 ♗b5

Now the path is cleared for the a-pawn to advance. Black is never able to move his own a-pawn for fear of dropping b6.
21...♖h7 22 a4 ♔c7 23 a5 ♖b8 24 0-0

With this White makes it possible for his other rook to get in on the action.
24...♖f7 25 axb6+ axb6 26 ♗c6!

It all seems so simple. Black dare not allow the white knight into d5 and so taking this bishop just isn't an option.

26...♖a8 27 ♕b5

Now the queen wants in on c6.
27...♕b8 28 ♘g4

It is amazing just how much

112

White's remaining knight gets around. Now it eyes up f6 and h6.
28...♞f8
Hardly inspirational but Black is completely tied up.
29 ♖fb1 ♞d7 30 ♗xd7 ♖xd7
Now White has a choice of pawns to take and the game is won.
31 ♗xf6 ♖xa1 32 ♖xa1 ♔c8 33 ♗h4 1-0
Black has had enough! Very clever chess.

Points
Anatoly 3
Boris 6
Chris 10
Dan 0
Elizabeth 4

Solution 1-7

As of yet this is not quite a 'Hedgehog' or a 'Maróczy Bind' scenario although it contains similarities of each. I'm not convinced that Black is actually threatening ...b7-b5 now although it could easily appear in the future.

Often in middlegames there isn't a best move, and just as with openings it could be down to a matter of taste. Perhaps someone might have suggested 18 b4 here to halt ...♞c5 although that would have involved weakening the c4-pawn. Basically I feel that all of our panel's suggestions are very plausible (well, possibly Anatoly's idea weakened a few squares and Boris was a little ambitious) although the game below should explain my bias.

Lalic-Krasenkow
European Club Cup, Neum 2000
18 ♞d5! ♗xb2 19 ♕xb2 b5
The knight is superbly placed on d5 but after 19...e6 20 ♞dc3 the d6-pawn is irrevocably weakened.
20 ♖ac1 bxc4 21 ♖xc4 ♞b6 22 ♞xb6 ♕xb6 23 ♞c3!
A second knight prepares to jump into d5.
23...♗d7?!
Perhaps Black should have accepted the pawn sacrifice, although 23...♕xe3+ 24 ♔h2 ♕a7 25 ♖c1! ♗d7 26 ♗xc6 ♗xc6 (or 26...♖xc6? 27 ♞d5 threatening mate!) 27 ♞d5 ♗xd5 28 ♖xc8 is a very favourable line for White.
24 ♖xd6!!
(see following diagram)
24...♕xe3+
The point of course was 24...exd6 25 ♞d5. With ♞f6+ in the air, this is the diagonal weakening that Dan was talking about.
25 ♔h2 ♞e5

If 25...♖fd8 then 26 ♖d1! with the simple threat of taking on c6.

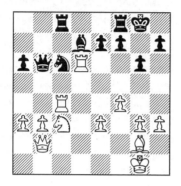

26 ♖xc8 1-0
The game might finish 26...♗xc8 (or 26...♖xc8 27 ♘d5) 27 ♘d5 ♘d3 28 ♘xe3 ♘xb2 29 ♖d2, when the knight is trapped.

Points
Anatoly 5
Boris 5
Chris 5
Dan 10
Elizabeth 6

Solution 1-8

Actually this is one of my own games and as far as I can recall, all five of our panel's suggestions were candidate moves for me.

When it came to analysing my options, the obvious 14 ♗d3 f5 15 ♕e2 c5 seemed to be okay for Black, whose life improves dramatically with the freeing of that b7-bishop. With that last line in mind, 14 h4 looked a little slow whilst 14 ♘e5 felt a bit mundane.

I saw the appeal of 14 c5!? bxc5 15 ♗d3 f5, which offers a pawn for some time, but there was nothing concrete. In truth it took me a while to spot (appropriately!) Chris's plan, but when I did I was really pleased with it and hence there was no hesitating.

Ward-Shulman
Isle of Man 2002
14 ♖e1! ♗b4 15 ♗d3 g6 16 ♖e3 ♕c8 17 ♗h6 ♖e8 18 ♘e5 ♗f8
Quite a cool variation is 18...c5 19 ♕f4 f6 20 ♘xg6! hxg6 21 ♗xg6 with a massive attack. The rook swinging along the third rank is a real bonus.
19 ♗xf8 c5
19...♘xf8 would not be dissimilar to the main game and 19...♖xf8 20 ♖h3 could also spell big trouble down the h-file.
20 ♕h4 ♘xf8 21 ♘g4
I liked the game continuation, although strictly speaking 21 ♕f6! would have been even stronger.
21...♘d7 22 ♘h6+ ♔g7 23 ♘xf7!

23...cxd4

If 23...♔xf7 then 24 ♕xh7+ ♔f6 (or 24...♔f8 25 ♗xg6) 25 ♕xg6+ ♔e7 26 ♖xe6+ ♔d8 27 ♖xe8+.

24 ♘d6 dxe3 25 ♘xc8 ♖axc8 26 ♕d4+ ♘f6 27 f3 e5 28 ♕xe3

and White went on to win.

Points

Anatoly 4
Boris 4
Chris 10
Dan 6
Elizabeth 4

Solution 1-9

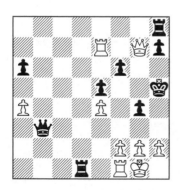

Chris does have a tendency to waffle sometimes (where have I heard that one before?), and in fact 36 ♖d7 ♖xf1+ 37 ♔xf1 ♕c4+ 38 ♔e1 ♕xe4+ is a ridiculous route to take. I also can't see a win after 36 ♖xe5+ fxe5 37 ♕xe5+ ♔g6 38 ♕f5+ ♔h6 39 ♕f6+ ♔h5, but at least White has a draw. The same is probably true of 36 ♕f7+ ♕xf7 37 ♖xf7 ♖d6, although White should beware 38 ♖c1? ♖c8!, taking the initiative due to the back rank threats.

Only White can be worse after 36 g3 ♖xf1+ 37 ♔xf1 ♕b1+ 38 ♔g2 ♕xe4+, and by a process of elimination full marks go to Anatoly. Actually this position occurred in a real game and this is how it ended:

Gaprindashvili-Veroci
Belgrade 1974
36 h3! ♖xf1+ 37 ♔h2

Obviously White's idea, which is certainly preferable to 37 ♔xf1?? ♕d1 mate.

37...g3+

Instead 37...♖h1+ 38 ♔xh1 ♕b1+ 39 ♔h2 ♕xe4 40 ♕xf6 ♕f4+ 41 ♕xf4 exf4 42 ♖e5+ ♔g6 43 hxg4 would reach a hopeless rook and pawn ending.

38 fxg3 ♕e3

(see following diagram)

39 ♕f7+? ♔h6 40 ♕g7+ ½-½

White evidently overlooked the pretty finish 39 ♖xe5+!! fxe5 40 g4+ ♔h4 41 ♕e7+ ♕g5 42 g3 mate.

115

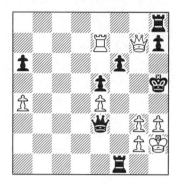

Points

Anatoly 10
Boris 3
Chris 0
Dan 3
Elizabeth 0

Solution 1-10

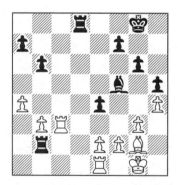

Anatoly was definitely having an off day when he made his suggestion and Boris's claim is more standard. However one must always beware of generalisations and take each position on its own merits. There is certainly no point in trying to trade off the passive e1-rook whilst 35...⬛dd2 can be met here with 36 ⬛e3, attacking the e-pawn.

Dan's idea would be fine if he could guarantee winning both of the queenside pawns, but after 35...⬛e6 36 ⬛xe4 ⬛xb3 37 ⬛c6 it's far from clear that he can do that.

In truth Black stands better after each of the suggestions although I am surprised that nobody came up with 35...⬛g7. Centralising the king is always (well nearly always!) a useful thing to do in the endgame and it isn't so easy for White to do that here.

Still, by far the most convincing suggestion is that of Elizabeth. On b4 a rook can attack and defend (both e4 and b6) at the same time. This was borne out in an encounter between two masters of old:

Levenfish-Botvinnik
Moscow/Leningrad 1937
35...⬛d4! 36 ⬛e3
If 36 ⬛c7 then simply 36...a5. The b3-pawn would remain doomed.
36...⬛b4 37 ⬛c1 ⬛2xb3 38 ⬛xb3 ⬛xb3 39 ⬛c4 ⬛b1+ 40 ⬛h2 ⬛b2 41 ⬛f1 0-1

Let's face it, there was hardly much to this question and it should have been an easy one.

Points

Anatoly 0
Boris 5
Chris 4
Dan 4
Elizabeth 10

Solutions To Test Two

Solution 2-1

All of our panel must be commended on their thoughts, although Black has no more than a draw by perpetual after 26...♘xa4 27 bxa4 ♗xa4 28 ♕xa4 ♕c3+ 29 ♔d1. I would have thought that 26...♗h3 (with the same idea of ...♘d7) would be more useful than 26...♗e8, while it is difficult to knock activating the a8-rook. Nevertheless, take a look at the following game:

V.Kovacevic-Seirawan
Wijk aan Zee 1980
26...♕h8! 27 f4

The forthcoming pin is inevitable as there is no time to run away, e.g. 27 ♔d2 ♕h4 28 ♖g2 ♗h3 and Black bags serious material.

27...♕h4 28 ♖d1 f6 29 gxf6 exf6 30 e5

White tries to make something happen before Black homes in on this file.

30...fxe5 31 fxe5 ♖f8

Alas, the f-file is even more rosy a prospect!

32 exd6+ ♔b7 33 ♗d3 ♖e8+ 0-1

Chris really is a clever boy!

Points
Anatoly 7
Boris 6
Chris 10
Dan 2
Elizabeth 3

Solution 2-2

In this tactical puzzle, first up we have 55 f8♘+ (I assume that's what Boris had in mind) 55...♚e7 56 ♘g6+ ♚e6 57 ♖e8+ (or 57 ♘f8+ ♚d5 58 ♖d8+ ♚c4) 57...♚f7 and White runs out of checks.

Upon 55 e6+ ♚xe6 56 ♘g5+ ♚d5 57 ♖d8+ ♚c4 58 f8♕ ♕c1+, it is Black who holds the initiative (and two extra pawns!). Regarding Chris's suggestion of 55 ♚f5 ♕f1+ 56 ♚g6 ♖c8 57 ♖xc8 ♚xc8 58 ♘g3. Well, White can dream on!

Certainly Elizabeth's 55 f8♕ ♕f1+ 56 ♚g3 ♕xf8 57 ♖xf8 offers some hope for a draw but it is Anatoly with the correct answer as was demonstrated in the following game:

Shulman-Ansell
Isle of Man 2002
55 ♖d8+! ♚xd8 56 f8♕+ ♚d7 57 ♘f6+ ♚e6 58 ♕g8+
(see following diagram)
58...♖f7
Or 58...♚e7 59 ♕e8 mate.

59 ♕c8+ ♚e7
The only alternative is the equally unappealing 59...♖d7 60 ♕xd7 mate.
60 ♕e8 mate (1-0)

Points
Anatoly 10
Boris 0
Chris 1
Dan 1
Elizabeth 3

Solution 2-3

Frankly, 22 ♘c3? ♘xc3 23 ♕xc3 ♕xd1 24 ♖xd1 ♖xd1 is simply better for Black (obviously he must be careful but the two rooks are better than the queen), and 22 ♗xd5 ♛xd5 23 ♛xd5 ♗xd5 24 ♘c3 ♗f3 leaves Black with the upper hand because with pawns on both sides, the bishop outclasses the knight.

I will award points for the contributions of Anatoly and Chris, but Elizabeth's straightforward continuation has been proven to be correct, as the following game shows:

Smyslov-Sanguinetti
Mar del Plata 1962
22 ♛h4 ♛e7

Upon 22...♔h7 23 ♘c3 there is no satisfactory way to escape the pin.
23 ♛xh6 b5 24 ♖d4!

After 24 ♘b2 ♘c3 the relative activity of the knights offers some compensation for the pawn. White need not worry about the knight just yet in view of the mating threats down the h-file.
24...♛f6 25 ♖h4 ♛g7 26 ♛xg7+

♔xg7 27 ♘c5
And so White has secured a free pawn.
27...♘c3 28 ♖c1 ♘xa2? 29 ♖c2 1-0

Points
Anatoly 5
Boris 0
Chris 5
Dan 0
Elizabeth 10

Solution 2-4

Unlike the last question this truly was a tough puzzle! There was no getting away from having to calculate variations:

a) 1...♛g4 2 ♗d2 and there is nothing doing, e.g. 2...♛d4 3 ♗c3 ♛d1 4 ♗e4.

b) 1...♛e5 2 ♗e3 ♛xb2 3 h3 and with so many squares covered White has nothing to fear.

c) 1...♛b4 2 ♖c1 ♖c5 (or 2...♖c7 3 ♛d1) 3 ♗c2 ♖c7 4 ♛d2 (with a back rank threat of his own) 4...f6 5 ♗b3! and suddenly White's threats are overwhelming. Here White's bishops get to show their true worth.

d) 1...♕d1 2 ♔f1 ♕h5 3 ♗d2 ♕xh2 (or 3...♕b5+ 4 ♔g1 ♕xb2 5 ♗e3) 4 f3. Essentially, unless Black has something especially good in store, a rook and two pawns (despite totalling seven points) isn't really better than the six points of a bishop pair. That's my opinion and I'm sticking to it!

So by process of elimination we come to the extremely well calculated game continuation:

Lagunov-Krasenkow
Dnepropetrovsk 1985
1...♕a4! 2 ♗d2
If 2 b3 then the cunning 2...♕a5!! would pick up the bishop on g5.
2...♖d6!
Creating the threat 3...♕d7. Now White actually played 3 ♔f1 and then resigned after 3...♕b5+ in view of 4 ♔g1 ♕d7. Let's see what happens if White is more resilient.
3 ♕e2 ♕d4!

Extremely clever. The queen returns to its original position.
4 ♗e1
Or 4 ♕b5 ♖d8 5 ♗e1 ♕d1 6 ♕a5 b6, when the b1-bishop is a goner.
4...♕d1 5 ♕e4 f5
and Black wins.

Points

Anatoly 10
Boris 2
Chris 2
Dan 4
Elizabeth 4

Solution 2-5

Elizabeth's comments are relevant as both 19 ♘a4 and 19 ♘e4 are annoyingly well met by 19...♘b4. Unfortunately, the concession of the b3-square is the drawback of 19 a3.

I don't buy into the 19 ♘xd5 concept as this de-isolates Black's c-pawn whilst leaving the d4-pawn as an obvious target. Furthermore, Black's major pieces will be able to pile up against White's b-pawn. I am

120

inclined to reward Dan's way of thinking but my top score goes to Boris based on the following game:

Matveeva-H.Hunt
Yerevan Women's Olympiad 1996
19 ♘g3! ♛b4 20 b3 ♛a5 21 ♛d2 ♖fd8 22 ♘xd5 ♛xd5 23 ♛e1 ♝b7

The key feature of this game is just how much Black's bishop is impaired by the presence of the pawn on c6.
24 ♖c5 ♛d7 25 f4!

Black's c- and e-pawns are going nowhere and hence neither is the bishop.
25...♛e7 26 ♛e5 f6 27 ♛e1 ♖d5 28 ♘e4 ♖e8 29 b4 ♛d8 30 ♛f2 e5 31 fxe5 fxe5 32 ♖f1 ♝a6 33 ♛f7+ ♚h8 34 ♖xd5 cxd5 35 ♘d6 ♖g8 36 ♛g6 ♖f8 37 ♘f7+ ♚g8 38 ♘xh6+ ♚h8 39 ♘f7+ ♚g8 40 ♛xa6 ♖xf7 41 ♛e6 ♛d7 42 ♛xf7+ ♛xf7 43 ♖xf7 ♚xf7 44 dxe5 ♚e6 45 ♚f2 ♚xe5 46 ♚e3 1-0

Points
Anatoly 2
Boris 10
Chris 3
Dan 6
Elizabeth 4

Solution 2-6

Accurate analysis is required but actually some lines aren't that long:
a) 16...e6 17 ♝xg7 ♚xg7 18 ♛h6+ ♚g8 19 f4 ♛c7 20 e5 dxe5 21 ♘e4 and the f6-knight is decisively removed. Sorry Anatoly, White doesn't even need to bother with the likes of ♘db5.
b) 16...♝xh6 17 ♛xh6 ♖xc3. A standard concept but, alas, here White isn't forced to recapture as he has bigger fish to fry: 18 g5! ♘h5 19 ♖xh5 gxh5 20 ♖h1 and an arrival on h7 is imminent!
c) 16...♛a5 17 ♝xg7 ♚xg7 18 ♛h6+ ♚g8 19 ♘d5 ♖e8 20 g5 ♘h5 21 ♖xh5 gxh5 22 ♘f6+ exf6 23 gxf6. It's safe to say that Elizabeth's idea is too casual.
d) 16...♖xd4 17 ♛xd4 and what

next Dan?

Well I suppose 16...♖xd4 and the unmentioned 16...♗h8 might postpone the mate threat, but by process of elimination you will see that it is Chris who has the best solution (he's a natural Dragon player!). Here's a practical example:

Wallace-Karlsson
Stockholm 1997
16...♘xe4 17 ♕e3

Upon 17 ♕h2 best is 17...♗e5! 18 ♗f4 (or 18 f4 ♗xd4) 18...♗xf4+ 19 ♕xf4 e5! 20 ♕h2 ♘g5.
17...♖xc3! 18 bxc3 ♘f6 19 ♗xg7 ♔xg7 20 ♖h2 ♖g8 21 ♘e2 ♔h8 22 ♘g3 ♗c6 23 c4 ♖g7

And with h7 now well protected, the black queen is free to go on the prowl.
24 ♕c3 ♔g8 25 c5 d5 26 ♘e4 ♘d7 27 ♘g5 e5 28 ♕d2 ♕e7 29 ♖dh1 ♘f8 30 f4 f6 31 ♘f3 ♕xc5 32 ♖f1 ♕a3+ 33 ♔b1 ♕a4 34 ♖hf2 ♕xf4 35 ♕xf4 exf4 36 ♘d4 g5 37 ♘f5 ♖c7 38 ♖e1 ♘g6 39 ♖e6 ♔f7 40 ♖d6 ♘e5 41
♘h6+ ♔g6 42 ♖h2 ♘f7 43 ♘f5 ♘xd6 44 ♖h6+ ♔f7 45 ♖xh7+ ♔e6 0-1

Points
Anatoly 2
Boris 4
Chris 10
Dan 2
Elizabeth 1

Solution 2-7

Anatoly's 31 g4?? is a rare blunder as it leaves the f3-knight en prise. Note that the a8-h1 diagonal is the only feature that White needs to worry about in his quest for advancement.

31 ♖g4?? hxg4? does work but 31...♕xd7 foils that idea! Dan has only come up with a drawing line whilst Chris has an interesting plan that could easily work. Full marks to Elizabeth, though, with a now famous game going very much according to plan:

Short-Timman
Tilburg 1991
31 ♔h2! ♖c8

Black must remain passive since 31...♗c8 allows 32 g4! (the bishop and queen are no longer aligned on the b7-g2 diagonal) 32...hxg4 (or 32...♗xd7 33 gxh5) 33 ♘g5! ♗xd7 34 h5! with a crushing attack.

Now White has an excellent offensive position but the immobility of the knight on f3 prevents an immediate knockout. However, English Grandmaster Nigel Short and our only female panellist both now find a phenomenal idea to use the king in the quest for checkmate.
32 ♔g3! ♖ce8 33 ♔f4! ♗c8 34 ♔g5! 1-0

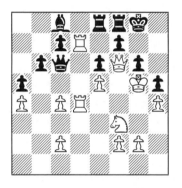

Black resigned in view of 35 ♔h6 and ♕g7 mate.

Points
Anatoly 0
Boris 0
Chris 6
Dan 2
Elizabeth 10

Solution 2-8

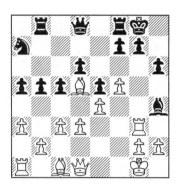

Gee, this really was points for old rope. Quite probably all roads (well, the ones taken by our panel) lead to Rome and I can only award them the way I see fit based on the following encounter:

Gaponenko-Agababean
European Women's Championship, Istanbul 2003
20 ♗xh6!

The most emphatic.
20...♗xg3

20...♗f6 would have been met by 21 ♕g4.
21 ♕g4 ♕f6 22 ♗g5 ♕xg5 23 ♕xg5 ♗f4 24 ♕g6 1-0

Points
Anatoly 4
Boris 2
Chris 8
Dan 10
Elizabeth 5

Solution 2-9

I know I said that it may be down to a matter of taste but I have to award points as I see fit. Anyway, I'm not too enamoured with Elizabeth's plan and although I certainly sympathise with Dan, it looks a little slow in view of 11 ♘c3 ♗g7 12 f4 0-0 13 ♘f3 ♖e8 - the e-pawn comes under fire too quickly for my liking.

Deviating from Dan is Anatoly's 12 ♗c4 0-0 13 ♘ge2, but after 13...♘bd7, my opinion is that the light-squared bishop is awkwardly placed and will be hassled, for example, by ...♘e5.

Clearly the move 11 ♘c3 can't be faulted but I have my reservations about 12 g4 0-0 13 h4. Too many pawn moves.

Take a look at the following encounter:

McShane-Wojtaszek
World Junior Championship, Goa 2002
11 ♘e2! ♗g7 12 ♘ec3 0-0 13

♗e2 ♘bd7 14 0-0 a6 15 a4

White will have plenty of pieces hindering the black break ...b7-b5.

15...♖b8 16 ♔h1 ♕d8 17 ♗e3 ♖e8 18 ♘a3 h6 19 ♕d2 ♔h7 20 ♖ab1

Looking to play b2-b4. For now White is happy to hold the kingside and attack Black's queenside.

20...♘h5 21 g4 ♘hf6 22 h3 ♘e5 23 ♖f2 g5

Black wanted to dissuade f3-f4 but it is on its way anyhow.

24 f4 gxf4 25 ♗xf4 b5

25...♘fd7 26 g5 doesn't solve all the problems either.

26 axb5 axb5 27 ♘axb5 ♗a6 28 ♘a3

White has netted a pawn and is back to consolidate. Having said that, continuing the initiative on the kingside with 28 g5!? had something to be said for it too.

28...♗xe2 29 ♕xe2 ♘fd7 30 ♘c2 c4 31 ♗d2 ♔g8 32 ♖f5 ♘c5 33 g5 hxg5 34 ♖xg5 ♘g6 35 ♖g4 ♘d3 36 ♘e3 ♘de5 37 ♖g3 ♗f6 38 ♘f5 ♖b7 39 ♕h5 ♖ee7

Black offers the exchange but, given the knight's superb placing, White isn't interested.

40 h4! ♘d3 41 ♕f3 ♗xc3 42 ♗xc3 ♖xe4 43 h5 ♖h4+

If 43...♖f4 then 44 hxg6! ♖xf3 45 ♘h6+ ♔f8 46 g7+ ♔e7 47 ♖xf3 hitting f7 as well as threatening a promotion and a variety of other things!

44 ♘xh4 ♕xh4+ 45 ♔g1 ♘df4 46 ♖e1 1-0

Actually, being a configuration that I have employed myself before, you may gather from this that I'm going with Chris for the top score!

Points

Anatoly 4
Boris 4
Chris 10
Dan 4
Elizabeth 2

Solution 2-10

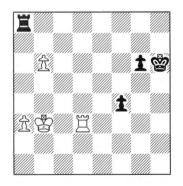

It is entirely possible that 46 a4 g5 47 ♔b4 g4 48 a5 g3 49 b7 ♖f8

(or 49...♖b8 50 a6 g2 51 ♖d1 f3 52 ♔a5 f2 53 a7 ♖xb7 54 a8♕ f1♕) 50 a6 g2 51 ♖d1 f3 52 a7 f2 53 b8♕ f1♕ is winning for White, so I'm going to award plenty of points for the logical concept of simply advancing the pawns. This position is based on an important tussle of my own, and to be honest I can't remember whether I figured out some defence for Black or I just got plain confused!

Certainly 46 ♖f3 is hardly a winning attempt in view of 46...♖b8, whilst 46 b7 ♖b8 47 ♖d7 f3 48 ♔c4 f2 49 ♖f7 ♖xb7 50 ♖xf2 would also be a draw. Note that 46 ♔b4 g5 47 ♔c5 g4 48 b7 ♖b8 49 ♔c6 f3 50 ♔c7 ♖xb7+ 51 ♔xb7 f2 would be rather embarrassing.

Although unusual, I was very pleased with my calculations:

Ward-McShane
British Championship, Torquay 2002
46 ♔c2! g5 47 b7 ♖b8 48 ♖b3 g4 49 ♔d2 ♔g5 50 ♔e2 f3+

Or 50...♔h4 51 ♔f2 g3+ 52 ♔g2 ♔g4 53 ♖b4!, when the a-pawn is free to do its thing!

51 ♔f2 ♔f4 52 ♖b4+ ♔e5 53 a4 ♔d6 54 a5 ♔c7 55 a6

(see following diagram)

The tempi situation has worked out perfectly for White.

55...g3+

With a6-a7 imminent, Black tries desperate tactics. Alas, nothing works for him.

56 ♔xg3 ♖g8+ 57 ♔xf3 ♔b8 58 ♖e4 ♔a7 59 ♖e6

Now the icing on the cake is to advance the king up the board in order to facilitate ♖e8.

59...♖f8+ 60 ♔g4 ♖g8+ 61 ♔f5 ♖d8 62 ♔f6 ♖f8+ 63 ♔g7 ♖d8 64 ♔f7 ♖d7+ 65 ♖e7 ♖d1 66 ♖e8 ♖f1+ 67 ♔g6 ♖g1+ 68 ♔h5 ♖g8 69 ♖xg8 1-0

Points

Anatoly 1
Boris 8
Chris 2
Dan 0
Elizabeth 10

Solutions To Test Three

Solution 3-1

Some may feel that I am splitting hairs with this one but I don't quite see it that way. I was very convinced by the treatment of this position by an ex-Soviet champion:

R.Hernandez-Psakhis
Calcutta 1988
29...♚b4! 30 ♗xc6
Or 30 ♖xc6 ♖hc8. I'm sure that White's precarious back rank situation didn't escape your attention.
30...♖hc8 31 ♖b1+ ♚c3 32 ♗b5 ♚d2! 33 g3 ♖c1+ 34 ♖xc1 ♚xc1 35 ♚g2 ♚d2 36 g4 g5 37 ♗c6 ♖b2 38 ♚g3 f6 39 ♗d7 e5 40 ♗b5 ♚e1 41 f4 exf4+ 42 exf4 ♖b3+ 43 ♚g2 gxf4 44 ♗c6 ♚e2 45 a5 f3+ 0-1

There was still a bit of work to be done once a pair of rooks were exchanged but there is no doubt that it makes Black's life a lot easier. After 29...♚d6 30 ♖xc6+ ♚e7 or 29...♚b6 30 ♖xc6+ ♚b7 31 ♖c1! the white rook lives to fight another day or at the very least make a bit of a nuisance of itself.

Generally speaking, if you have a rook (and hopefully a pawn or two) for two minor pieces then you should seek to trade off the opponent's remaining rook, and if you are the exchange down (hopefully for a pawn or two) then you should try to preserve your lone rook.

Possibly Anatoly has got a point (so I'll give him more than that!) but one may as well take the easy route.

Points

Anatoly 4
Boris 3
Chris 10
Dan 3
Elizabeth 4

Solution 3-2

(see following diagram)
Boris is right to say that White holds the initiative on both sides of the board, but the rest of his solu-

127

tion is fantasy. I also don't feel that there is any need to swap off the rooks yet. I suppose that the debate that Anatoly and Chris are having is whether in gearing for an h-file invasion, Black can break on the queenside (presumably with ...b7-b6). I'm going to award points to both of those guys but the top score goes to Dan.

cramped conditions.

Points
Anatoly 5
Boris 0
Chris 6
Dan 10
Elizabeth 2

Solution 3-3

Capablanca-Treybal
Karlsbad 1929
36 b5 axb5 37 h6+ ♔f8 38 axb5 ♔e7 39 b6 ♕b8 40 ♖a1 ♖c8 41 ♕b4 ♖hd8 42 ♖a7 ♔f8 43 ♖h1 ♗e8 44 ♖ha1 ♔g8 45 ♖1a4 ♔f8 46 ♕a3 ♔g8 47 ♔g3 ♗d7 48 ♔h4 ♔h8 49 ♕a1 ♔g8 50 ♔g3 ♔f8 51 ♔g2 ♗e8 52 ♘d2 ♗d7 53 ♘b3 ♖e8 54 ♘a5 ♘d8 55 ♗a6 bxa6 56 ♖xd7 ♖e7 57 ♖xd8+ ♖xd8 58 ♘xc6 1-0

This old game was a joy to watch. It's amazing just how much damage can be done through the domination of only one file when the opponent is having to operate under such

I would really love to award the points to Elizabeth but although I will give her answer something, unfortunately there is a more accurate one out there. Boris would have to be careful that he isn't losing after 41 ♖exd3 exd3 42 ♖xd3 ♖e4+ 43 ♔b5 ♖xg4 as connected passed pawns are extremely dangerous in endgames.

Without keeping you in suspense, it is Dan who takes home the bacon.

Mista-Aseev
Cappelle la Grande 2003
41 ♖dxd3! exd3 42 ♖xe5 fxe5 43 ♔c3
Here Black resigned in view of

128

43...e4 44 a5

Yes, the black king is outside of 'the square'. Sorry if you think that was a trick question, but you should remain on the ball at all times!

Points
Anatoly 3
Boris 0
Chris 3
Dan 10
Elizabeth 4

Solution 3-4

Do up your seatbelt and then play over the following encounter:

Polgar-Berkes
Budapest 2003
12 ♗h7+! ♚h8 13 ♗e4 hxg5

Upon 13...♖b8 14 h4! the line 14...hxg5 15 hxg5+ ♚g8 16 ♗h7+ ♚h8 17 ♕f4, which would see the queen coming to the h-file to deliver mate, highlights the use of having the move ...♚h8 forced upon the opponent.

14 g4!!

White's ingenious idea! Now the rook on a8 remains under attack and Black is defenceless against the opening of the h-file. Note that White gave no thought to 14 ♗xa8? g4 which, in view of ...♗g5, would have secured a second piece for the rook.

14...♖b8 15 h4 g6

Observe 15...gxh4 16 g5 ♚g8 17 ♕f4 f5 18 ♕xh4 fxe4 19 ♕h7+ ♚f7 20 ♕h5+ g6 21 ♕h7+ ♚e8 22 ♕xg6+ ♖f7 23 ♖h7.

16 hxg5+ ♚g7 17 ♕f4 ♗b7

17...♖h8 18 ♖xh8 ♕xh8 19 ♘e5 ♘xe5 20 ♕xe5+ ♚g8 21 ♕xc7 was no better.

18 ♖h7+! ♔xh7 19 ♕h2+ ♔g8 20
♖h1 ♗xg5+ 21 ♘xg5 ♕xg5+ 22
f4 ♕xf4+

Forced!

23 ♕xf4 ♗xe4 24 ♕xe4 1-0

Very impressive and my justification for awarding the top marks
to Anatoly.

Boris has a thematic idea too and
in fact I'm going to be generous as
there were plenty of very plausible
suggestions. (Actually Dan, I'm a bit
worried about that knight and the
b7-h1 diagonal!)

Points

Anatoly 10
Boris 7
Chris 3
Dan 1
Elizabeth 4

Solution 3-5

When it comes to chess (I
couldn't vouch for anything else!),
Grandmaster Bogdan Lalic has a
mind full of useful information.
Though again all of the suggestions

have at least some appeal, Mr Lalic
told me that he was extremely
pleased with his plan in the following game:

B.Lalic-Hulak
Croatian Championship 1995

15 ♗a6!?

By the way, Bogdan felt that
Black's kingside defences were
pretty solid and that could have
influenced his leaning toward this.

15...♗xa6 16 ♕xa6 ♔g7

I'm not arguing with Bogdan, but
having studied this game I do feel
that really Black should have played
16...♕c8!? here. White won't trade
queens but by then parking the
queen on b7, Black can at least help
plug that hole on c6 and allow his
rooks to challenge for the c-file.
Now the rest is very instructive.

17 ♖ed1 ♕b8 18 g3 ♗d6 19
♗xf6+ ♘xf6 20 ♘b5

White's pieces are very comfortable on the weakened light squares
a6 and b5. Meanwhile, with White
intending complete domination of
the c-file, Black has but one safe
square available for the queen.

20...♘d5 21 a3 ♖d8 22 ♖c6

The invasion begins on this natural entry point.

22...♘e7 23 ♖c4

Kicked away but still ready to
double.

23...h6 24 ♖dc1 g5

This looks a bit desperate but
what else is Black to do?

25 ♘d2 ♘d5 26 ♘e4 ♗e7 27

♘ec3!

Preparing to swap off Black's only truly well placed piece.
27...♘xc3 28 ♖1xc3

Now ♖c7 is looming and White is rubbing his hands in glee with the thought of that seventh rank!
28...e5 29 d5 e4 30 ♖xe4 ♗f6 31 ♖d3 ♗xb2 32 d6 ♖e8 33 ♖de3 ♖xe4 34 ♖xe4 ♕c8 35 ♕xc8 ♖xc8 36 ♘xa7 ♖c1+

Finally Black has got active but it is too little too late.
37 ♔g2 ♖d1 38 ♘b5 ♔f6 39 ♖c4 ♖c1 40 ♖b4 ♗e5 41 f4 gxf4 42 gxf4 ♖c2+ 43 ♔f3 ♗b2 44 h4 ♖d2 45 ♔e4 ♔e6 46 f5+ ♔f6 47 ♘c7 ♖e2+ 48 ♔d3 ♗xa3 49 ♔xe2 1-0

So I've awarded ten points to Chris for that little bit extra. Anatoly and Elizabeth suffer the most as 16 a4 concedes the b4-square and just looks a little odd (I knew you'd love my grandmasterly explanations!), whilst 16 ♘e4 encourages too many trades for my liking. I'm

not saying that's necessarily going to happen, but theoretically speaking, the more pieces that are swapped off, the weaker the 'IQP' becomes.

Points

Anatoly 3
Boris 6
Chris 10
Dan 6
Elizabeth 3

Solution 3-6

Regarding 37 f4 ♗xg3 38 ♔xg3 ♕g1+ 39 ♔f3 (or 39 ♕g2 ♕xe3+) 39...♕h1+, don't call us Dan, we'll call you! It is my opinion (and I'm not the only one) that in view of the activity of the black queen, after both 37 ♕c6 and 37 ♕d5 the queen ending that arises from 37...♗xg3 is drawn.

Hence the knight must be preserved but the problem with 37 ♘f1 is 37...♕b2!, when White has a lot of difficulty defending f2. The late Tony Miles foresaw this problem and as a result came up with an outrageous solution that most wouldn't even have considered, let alone played!

Miles-Makarichev
Oslo 1984
37 ♘h1 ♛b2 38 ♛c6
It would be an understatement to say that knights aren't renowned for their strengths when operating in a corner of the board. However, the English Grandmaster understood that this position wasn't about attacking the black king. No, the knight holds the fort at the back, leaving the queen free to go on the prowl. Note the white queen dominates the centre whilst the black queen, possibly in its search for activity, has actually been caught offside. Furthermore, though it has more scope than the knight, the 'bad' bishop now becomes a mere bystander.
36...♛b1 39 ♛xc7 ♛e4+ 40 ♔h2 h5 41 ♛c6 ♛c2 42 gxh5 ♛f5 43 ♛g2 ♛xh5 44 c5 bxc5 45 b6 ♛d1 46 ♛c6 ♝e7 47 ♘g3 c4 48 b7 ♝d6 49 ♘e4 ♝b8 50 ♛c8 ♛f3 51 ♛xb8 ♛xe4 52 ♛c7 ♛f3 53 ♔g1 ♛d1+ 54 ♔g2 ♛d5+ 55 ♔g3 1-0

Points
Anatoly 3
Boris 3
Chris 4
Dan 0
Elizabeth 10

3-7

Upon 15...f5? the capture 16 exf6 would leave a gaping hole on g6, and for that matter the sacrifice 16 ♘xd5!? exd5 17 ♛xd5 may be very powerful too. Too many holes are created after 15...g5?! and with 16 ♘e2 the white knights can prepare to invade some of them.

However, that is the end of Black's bad news in a game in which I personally learned an awful lot. In fact, I would definitely cite the following encounter as the one in which I have received the biggest chess lesson in the last few years. Coincidentally, upon reaching this position, my views mirrored those of Chris (fancy that!). I can remember that gradually over the board I discovered that in fact things weren't that great at all as after 15...b5! I seemed to have little more to do. I had been waiting (and continued to do so) for my chance to align the queen and bishop along the b1-h7 diagonal, but the reality is that such a kingside attack is not the same without the presence of a dark-squared bishop. For one thing, when White has a dark-squared bishop Black can't play ...g6 to thwart a mate on h7 with a pawn already on h6. That kind of sounds greedy since only that piece and one pawn has disappeared from White's army. However, later super-GM Nigel Short explained why in similar French Defence scenarios White's dark-squared bishop can be just as valuable as its partner despite the presence of white pawns on dark squares.

Ward-Psakhis
Isle of Man 1999
1 d4 e6 2 ♘f3 ♘f6 3 ♗g5 c5 4 c3 h6 5 ♗xf6 ♕xf6 6 e4 cxd4 7 cxd4 ♗b4+ 8 ♘c3 ♘c6 9 ♖c1 d5 10 e5 ♕d8 11 a3 ♗e7 12 ♗d3 ♗d7 13 b4 ♖c8 14 0-0 a6 15 ♕b3 b5! 16 ♘e2 ♕b6 17 ♖c3 0-0 18 ♗b1 g6 19 ♖fc1 a5! 20 ♖c5!?

I didn't want to allow the black knight into c4 and with little else to do about my b-pawn, I saw this as a good practical try. If Black takes the exchange then he will be a little weak on the dark-squares, although as I highlight above, it's not as though I have retained that particular bishop!

20...axb4 21 axb4 ♖a8 ½-½

To say I was relieved by the draw offer was an understatement

and the watching Nigel Short was also very surprised. 'Black stands better,' he declared and in retrospect, I'm definitely not going to argue with him! Black could soon be ready to grab that exchange.

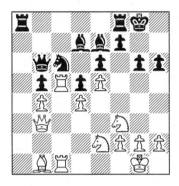

Points
Anatoly 2
Boris 10
Chris 3
Dan 0
Elizabeth 4

Solution 3-8

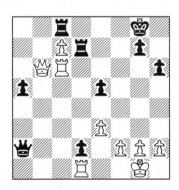

The key move for White to look out for is 30...♕a4, which would hit both the c6-rook and the last line of defence on d1. Checking on analysis we have:

a) 30 ♕b7 (I don't see why 30 ♕b8 shouldn't transpose) 30...♕a4!! (a cute variation is 30...♕a1? 31 ♕xc8+ ♔h7 32 ♖xh6+! ♔xh6 33 ♕h8+ ♔g6 34 ♕e8+ ♔h6 35 ♕e6+ ♔h7 36 ♕h3+ ♔g6 37 ♕g4+ ♔h7 38 ♖xa1 which does win for White thanks to the cover of d1) 31 ♕xc8+ ♔h7 32 h3! ♕xc6 (and not 32...♕xd1+? 33 ♔h2) 33 ♖xd2 ♕c1+ 34 ♔h2 ♕xd2 35 ♕b8 ♖xc7 36 ♕xc7 ♕d5, which only leaves Black with winning chances (though it should be drawn).

b) 30 ♖d6 ♕c2. Well that was easy!

c) 30 g3 ♕a4! 31 ♕b8 (unfortunate is 31 ♖xd2 ♖xd2 32 ♕b7 ♕d1+ 33 ♔g2 ♖xf2+! 34 ♔xf2 ♖f8+ 35 ♔g2 ♕f1 mate; one can see why the white monarch is better off on h2 than on g2) 31...♕xd1+ 32 ♔g2 ♖dxc7.

Unfortunately for Boris's namesake, Korchnoi played the most accurate move.

Korchnoi-Spassky
Belgrade 1977
30 h3!! ♕a4 31 ♖xd2! ♖xd2 32 ♕b7 ♖dd8 33 cxd8♕+ ♖xd8 34 ♖c7!
(see following diagram)
And suddenly it's seventh heaven for White, whose own king is as safe as houses.
34...♕a1+ 35 ♔h2 e4 36 ♕xe4

♕f6 37 f4 ♕f8 38 ♖a7 ♕c5 39 ♕b7 ♕c3 40 ♕e7 ♖f8 41 e4 ♕d4 42 f5 h5 43 ♖xa5 ♕d2 44 ♕e5 ♕g5 45 ♖a6 ♖f7 46 ♖g6 ♕d8 47 f6 h4 48 fxg7 1-0

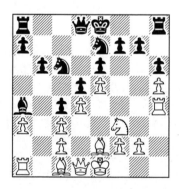

Points
Anatoly 0
Boris 10
Chris 0
Dan 2
Elizabeth 2

Solution 3-9

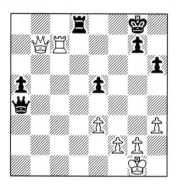

As we're only in the early stages of the middlegame of course, it might be reasonable to say that any plan Black adopts could be simply down to matter of taste. I'm not buying that argument here, though! It's full marks to Anatoly with a high-class practical encounter to justify my decision.

A.Sokolov-Yusupov
Riga 1986
13...♔d7 14 ♗e3 ♕g8 15 ♕d2 ♕h7

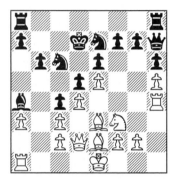

The black queen could have hovered around c7 and d7 but with so many fixed pawns in the centre it would never have got stuck into the game there. This manoeuvre, however, is an act of genius as all sorts of possibilities open up along the h7-c2 diagonal. It would be outrageous for me to claim that Black is winning as a result but the middlegame has certainly started off well. 16 ♖c1 ♔c7 17 ♖f4 ♖af8 18 ♘h4 ♘d8 19 ♗g4 ♔b7 20 ♖f3 ♗e8 21 ♖h3 g5 22 hxg6 fxg6 23 ♘f3 g5 24 ♘h2 ♕g7 25 ♕e2 ♗g6 26 ♗h5 ♘f5 27 ♔d2 ♗h7 28 ♘g4 ♘c6 29 ♘f6 ♖xf6 30 exf6

♕xf6 31 ♗g4 ♘d6 32 f3 ♗f5 33 ♗xf5 exf5 34 ♖ch1 f4 35 ♗f2 ♖e8 36 ♕d1 ♘f5 37 ♖e1 ♖e7 38 ♖hh1 ♔c7 39 a4 ♕f7 40 ♖xe7+ ♕xe7 41 ♖e1 ♕f7 42 ♕e2 ♔d7 43 ♔c1 h5 44 ♔b2 ♕g6 45 ♕f1 g4 46 ♖e2 g3 47 ♗e1 ♘fe7 48 ♗d2 ♕f5 49 ♕e1 h4 50 a5 bxa5 51 ♕a1 ♘g6 52 ♕a3 h3 53 gxh3 ♕h5 54 ♕c5 ♕xf3 55 ♖e1 ♘ge7 56 ♕b5 g2 57 ♕b7+ ♔d6 58 ♖g1 ♕f2 59 ♗xf4+ ♕xf4 60 ♖xg2 ♕f3 61 ♖g4 ♕xh3 62 ♖f4 ♔e6 63 ♖f8 ♕h6 64 ♖f3 ♕h8 65 ♖e3+ ♔d6 66 ♖f3 ♕h6 67 ♖f1 ♕g7 68 ♔a3 ♘f5 69 ♕c8 ♘e3 70 ♖f8 ♘xc2+ 71 ♔a4 ♘2xd4 72 cxd4 ♕xd4 0-1

Otherwise, I consider 13...0-0 to be a bit too provocative, and though the knight manoeuvre is kind of interesting, I'll give the second highest score to the solid 13...♕d7 and ...0-0-0 plan. Finally, a pawn might get in the way on b5, while ...a6-a5 and ...b5-b4 doesn't make much sense.

Points
Anatoly 10
Boris 2
Chris 4
Dan 3
Elizabeth 6

Solution 3-10
(see following diagram)
Anatoly had a couple of valid points which are proven after:

a) 71...g5+ 72 ♔f3. The white king now need not budge and the bishop can just oscillate along the h3-c8 diagonal. Yes, White will be more than happy to concede his bishop for the two black pawns after a future ...g5-g4+.

b) 71...gxf5 72 ♔xf5 ♗e1 73 ♔f4 (the king is heading for g2 and h1 via f3) 73...h4 74 ♔g4.

c) 71...♗g5+ 72 ♔e4 gxf5+ (or else ♗xg6 will follow next and the king can safely make it back to the light-squared corner) 73 ♔xf5.

However, there is clearly something that the real Mr Karpov managed to factor into the equation:

Anand-Karpov
Monaco (blind) 1994
71...♗g3+! 72 ♔e4

Obviously 72 ♔xg3 gxf5 is hopeless.
72...gxf5+ 73 ♔xf5 ♗b8 74 ♔e4
White begins his journey back, but is he going to make it?
74...h4 75 ♔f3 h3 76 ♔f2 ♗h2 0-1

I'm afraid 'no' is the answer! Regarding the white king setting up shop in the h1 corner, alas it's a case of so near yet so far, for example 77 ♔f3 ♔h5 78 ♔f2 ♔g4 79 ♔e2 ♔g3 80 ♔f1 ♔f3 81 ♔e1 ♗g1 82 ♔f1 h2.

Points
Anatoly 4
Boris 3
Chris 3
Dan 10
Elizabeth 2

Solutions To Test Four

Solution 4-1

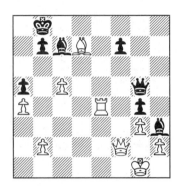

This was actually a game of my own and although at the time it seemed that there was nothing much riding on this encounter because my tournament wasn't going that well, I should have remembered that things can always get worse!

On general principles I really should have stuck to Elizabeth's advice. I could have double-checked any serious tactics after reaching the time control. Instead, though, this is what happened:

Ward-Marusenko
Isle of Man 2000
39 c6 ♗b6 40 ♖e8+?? ♚a7

and having made the time control I found myself with plenty of time to reflect upon the error of my ways and then tender my resignation!

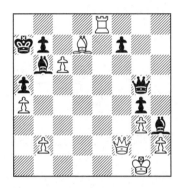

How could I have been so stupid as to allow that dark-squared bishop into the game? In fact I had got confused and if I had gone with Chris's deviation from the above with 40 c7+! ♚a7 (or 40...♗xc7 41 ♖c4+ ♚xd7 42 ♕xb6) then either a queen or a knight promotion would have justified my decision.

It always pays to look out for checks and neither 39 ♕f5? ♕c1+ 40 ♚f2 ♕f1+ 41 ♚e3 ♕c1+ 42 ♚d4 ♕d2+ 43 ♚c4 ♕c2+ with at least a draw by perpetual check, nor of course 39 ♕xf7?? ♕c1+ 40 ♚f2 ♕f1+, netting the queen, do that.

137

Points

Anatoly 1
Boris 0
Chris 10
Dan 0
Elizabeth 10

Yes, the first instance of me giving full marks for two answers. 40 c7+ would have been an emphatic finish but without a doubt it is better to be safe than sorry!

Solution 4-2

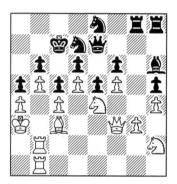

One must always try to remain objective but Elizabeth's opinion here demonstrates a lack of ambition. She might have a point about the g3-g4 break, though, and certainly 62 g4 ♗f4! looks a bit premature. Boris's idea has imagination, although obviously the black rooks couldn't be better placed. It is Anatoly who hits the jackpot:

Delchev-A.Hoffman
Linares 2003
62 ♗xa5! bxa5 63 b6+ ♔b7 64 ♖b5!

Now the white rooks can worm their way into the black position with the opponent's queenside-based pieces being bystanders.
64...♘g7 65 ♖xa5 ♖a8 66 ♖a7+!
♖xa7 67 bxa7+

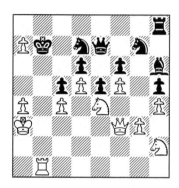

67...♔xa7

Upon 67...♔a8? 68 ♕b3, mate is imminent along the b-file.
68 ♕c3 ♔a6

If 68...♕d8 then after 69 ♘xd6 White threatens amongst other things the simple fork ♘f7.
69 ♖b5 ♕d8 70 ♘xd6

Black had to stop the mate on a5 and so this happens anyway.
70...♘e8 71 ♘f7 ♕c7 72 d6
♘xd6 73 ♘xd6 ♖b8 74 ♘e4 ♖d8
75 ♘f1 ♖b8 76 ♘h2 ♗f8 77 ♘f3
♘b6 78 ♘fd2 ♖d8 79 ♘b3 ♖d4
80 ♘exc5+ 1-0

Points

Anatoly 10
Boris 4
Chris 3
Dan 1
Elizabeth 2

Solution 4-3

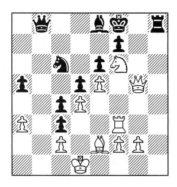

What on earth is Boris on about? He has clearly overlooked 28 ♖f4?? ♕b1 mate. Indeed, Black is on the verge of activating both his queen and his rook and I prefer the second player's position after 28 ♖xc3 ♘xd4 as White's centre is coming apart at the seams. Furthermore, the variation 28 ♖h3 ♕b1+ 29 ♕c1 ♕xc1+ 30 ♔xc1 ♖xh3 31 gxh3 ♘xd4 32 ♗d1 ♗a4 is also extremely promising for Black, thus explaining the stance that Anatoly has adopted.

It's not mate but Dan's suggestion is still the best:

Kovchan-Sadvakasov
Rector Cup, Kharkov 2003
28 ♘d7+! ♗xd7 29 ♖xf7+! ♔e8

White's intention was 29...♔xf7 30 ♕f6+ ♔g8 31 ♕g6+ ♔f8 32 ♕f6+ etc.

30 ♖f8+!! ♖xf8 31 ♗h5+ ♖f7 32 ♗xf7+ ♔xf7 ½-½

And thus White obtained a share of the wares thanks to the perpetual check. A draw is better than nothing!

Points
Anatoly 3
Boris 0
Chris 1
Dan 10
Elizabeth 4

Solution 4-4

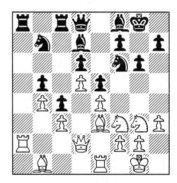

White has a space advantage and thus it makes a lot of sense to keep the pieces on the board - 24 ♗h6 hardly does that. Although Boris wants to somehow get in on g7, that is unlikely and he is simply offering his 'good' bishop for Black's 'bad' one.

Although h4-h5 does have some appeal, a big concession is the g4-square. Points are deserved for these options and both 24 ♗g5 and 24 ♘h2, but Anatoly Karpov's choice is absolutely inspired.

Karpov-Unzicker
Nice Olympiad 1974
24 ♗a7!

Guaranteeing for now the preservation of the rooks. There was a danger that Black would take control of the a-file but now White can double or even treble major pieces before they come into confrontation again. That, of course, would secure the first player the a-file. Note now how Black struggles to get by under such cramped circumstances, with the dreadful knight on b7 highlighting his plight.

24...♘e8 25 ♗c2 ♘c7 26 ♖ea1 ♕e7 27 ♗b1 ♗e8 28 ♘e2 ♘d8 29 ♘h2 ♗g7 30 f4 f6?

An ugly response, but although many would have captured on f4 in order to utilise the e5-square, the black knights are far away from that post.

31 f5 g5

Black appears to be trying to completely block up the position but his attempts are soon thwarted. However, retaining the tension wouldn't have been great either, for example 31...♗f7 32 ♘g3 ♘e8 33 ♕f2, when White could use the f-file as well as dominating the a-file and having the option to invade on b6.

32 ♗c2

This piece wasn't pulling its weight and with the square h5 in mind, Karpov sets about improving its position

32...♗f7 33 ♘g3 ♘b7 34 ♗d1 h6 35 ♗h5

Offering to trade off 'bad' for 'good' bishop. The less said about the one on g7 the better!

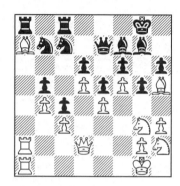

35...♕e8 36 ♕d1 ♘d8 37 ♖a3 ♔f8 38 ♖1a2

Now if desired White could actually treble his major pieces on the a-file.

38...♔g8 39 ♘g4 ♔f8

Of course not 39...♗xh5 40 ♘xh5 ♕xh5?? 41 ♘xf6+. The fact is that Black can do nothing but sit back and wait for the inevitable.

40 ♘e3 ♔g8 41 ♗xf7+ ♘xf7 42 ♕h5 ♘d8 43 ♕g6 ♔h8 44 ♘h5 1-0

Black has had enough and who can blame him? White is yet to flex his muscles on the a-file and given the inroads he has made on the kingside, he may not even need to.

Points
Anatoly 10
Boris 3
Chris 4
Dan 3
Elizabeth 5

Solution 4-5

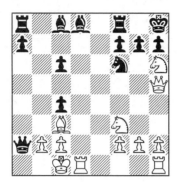

Sorry, I guess that my 'beware that all may not be as it seems' statement was a bit of a red herring. In fact, it's not really that difficult and by a process of elimination we have:

a) 19 ♖xd8?? ♕a1+ 20 ♔d2 ♖xd8+ 21 ♔e2 ♕xh1 and as well as the queen on h5, Black threatens 22...♕d1+.

b) 19 ♗xf6 ♗xf6 20 ♘xf7+ ♖xf7 21 ♕xf7 ♗f5 and White's king is in big trouble.

c) 19 ♘xf7+ ♔g8 and White has solved nothing.

d) 19 ♘g5 ♕a1+ 20 ♔d2 ♘xh5 21 ♘gxf7+ ♖xf7 22 ♘xf7+ ♔g8 23 ♘h6+ gxh6 24 ♖xa1 is quite visual, arguably White is worse.

White has a much better alternative, as seen in the following game:

Tal-Smyslov
Candidates Tournament, Belgrade 1959
19 ♕xf7! ♕a1+

Of course 19...♖xf7 20 ♖xd8+ leads to mate.
20 ♔d2 ♖xf7 21 ♘xf7+ ♔g8 22 ♖xa1 ♔xf7 23 ♘e5+ ♔e6 24 ♘xc6 ♘e4+ 25 ♔e3 ♗b6+ 26 ♗d4 1-0

Points
Anatoly 4
Boris 0
Chris 10
Dan 0
Elizabeth 0

Solution 4-6

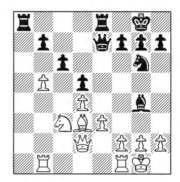

Oh Chris, Chris, Chris, what are you talking about? By parking a bishop on c6, that piece may look like a big pawn. However, as it isn't officially, Black will still have two isolanis!

White's way forward is much clearer after 18...♖ad8 19 bxc6 bxc6 20 ♗xg6!? hxg6 21 ♖b6 and I can't help feeling that 18...♖a3 isn't really coordinating Black's forces.

It is thematic for Black to get going on the kingside but 18...h5?!

19 ♗xg6 fxg6 20 bxc6 bxc6 just looks ugly. Also note 21 f3!? ♕xe3+ 22 ♕xe3 ♖xe3 23 ♘d1.

One would have to say that 18...♕g5 should be a candidate here too, but it is very difficult to argue with the game continuation:

Grabarczyk-Jakubowski
Polish Championship 2003
18...♘h4! 19 ♗e2?!

This doesn't seem to help but an investigation into the position shows the somewhat surprising strength of Black's offensive:

a) 19 ♖fc1?! ♗h3! 20 ♗f1 ♕g5. As well as the g2-pawn, Black threatens the fork on f3.

b) 19 ♔h1? ♘f3! 20 ♕c2 (or 20 gxf3 ♗xf3+ 21 ♔g1 ♕g5 mate) 20...h3 ♗xh3 with a forced mate.

c) 19 ♕c2 ♗h3! and g2 drops anyway.

d) 19 ♘e2 ♗h3! 20 ♘f4? ♗xg2!.
19...♗h3! 20 g3 ♕f6!

Of course Black could just take the exchange directly but in view of ...♘f3+ this is even better.

21 ♕d1

Obviously 21 ♖fc1 ♘f3+ 22 ♗xf3 ♕xf3 would invite a mate on g2.

21...♗xf1 22 ♗xf1 ♘f3+ 23 ♔g2 ♘g5 24 bxc6 bxc6 25 ♖b6 g6 26 ♘xd5?

Falling into Black's trap accelerates the defeat but the final result isn't in much doubt.

26...♕d8! 0-1

Oops, that's a piece!

Points

Anatoly 3
Boris 10
Chris 2
Dan 4
Elizabeth 4

Solution 4-7

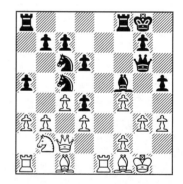

Not unusually, our panel have offered some valid arguments. Important features to note are that White is rather tied down to the defence of his d-pawn and, given the strength of the c5-knight, should probably be looking to kick it away via ♗d2 and b3-b4. With that in mind, I am convinced that the legend that is Bobby Fischer was spot on with his handling of this position:

Saidy-Fischer
New York 1969
18...♖a6! 19 ♗d2 ♖b6 20 ♗xa5

It's worth noting that 20 ♘a4 would have fallen foul of 20...♘xd3! and, that aside, there was no way to guard the b-pawn. Hence White dabbles in a little tactic in order to try and retain material equilibrium.
20...♖xb3

White's point was 20...♘xa5 21 b4, but Black has no need to go down that path.
21 ♗d2

The bishop is lost after 21 ♗xc7 ♖c8.
21...♖a8

The outcome of the last few moves then is that White has been saddled with an isolated a-pawn, a feature which Black immediately sets about exploiting.
22 a4 ♖a6!?

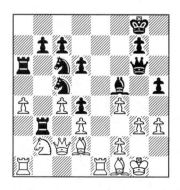

Amazing. As if like a re-run, the second rook prepares to swing to b6 in order to pressurise the awkwardly placed b2-knight.
23 a5 ♔h7

In fact after the immediate 23...b6 24 axb6 ♖axb6 25 ♖a8+ ♔h7, actually 26 ♖ee8 wouldn't have worked because of 26...♘b8!. Nevertheless, Fischer opts to avoid any potential backlash.
24 ♖ed1 b6 25 ♗e1

Suddenly White is completely passive. Observe the horrendous 25 axb6 ♖axb6 26 ♖ab1 ♘xd3.
25...bxa5 26 ♘a4 ♖xd3!

A temporary exchange sacrifice that leaves White hopelessly weak on the light squares.
27 ♗xd3 ♗xd3 28 ♕a2 ♘b4 29 ♕a3

With 29 ♕b2 ♘xa4 30 ♖xa4 ♗c2 another possibility, Black is destined to regain his material and some!
29...♘c2 30 ♕b2 ♘xa1 31 ♖xa1 ♘xa4 32 ♖xa4 ♕e4 33 ♗xa5 ♖xa5 34 ♖xa5 ♕e1+ 35 ♔h2 ♕xa5 36 ♕xd4 0-1

The truth is that I can't help but award points for other suggestions. Actually, I'm not that sure that 18...a4 19 b4 ♘b3 20 ♖b1 helps much as 21 ♘xa4 is in the air. Also, I have my doubts that 18...h4 19 g4 is a positive trade. True, 18...♖ae8 is very natural although 19 ♗d2 does carry with it the freeing b4 push. Still, with 18...♖ab8 not unreasonable too, I'm feeling generous!

Points
Anatoly 6
Boris 5
Chris 6
Dan 10
Elizabeth 4

Solution 4-8

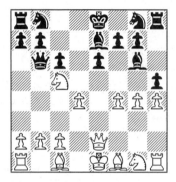

Crumbs, there really is a load of twaddle being spoken here and you should really be ashamed of yourself if you failed to locate the right answer. By a process of elimination:

a) 10 g5 ♗xc5 11 dxc5 ♕xc5 and Black is a pawn up with a firm grip on the f5-square.

b) 10 gxh5 ♖xh5 and White has two weak isolated kingside pawns and Black's firm grip on f5 tallies well with his simple threat to take on c5 as well as h4!

c) 10 ♖h3 (an interesting concept but quite frankly in this position it's not too hot!) 10...hxg4 11 ♖b3 ♗xh4+ 12 ♔d1 ♕d8 and, bearing in mind the attack on the d-pawn, White's position is a bit of a mess.

d) 10 ♘xe6? fxe6 and now what? Sorry Dan, but White can hardly justify offloading a piece with the vast majority of his army still resting on the back rank!

I suppose Anatoly's is the best of these four but Elizabeth's correct solution is in a class of its own. Take a look at the following game:

Rublevsky-Diepeveen
Berlin 1992
10 f5 exf5 11 g5 ♘d7 12 ♘b3 ♕c7

White has excellent compensation for what will only be one pawn after 12...♗f8 13 ♗e3 ♖e8 14 0-0-0 ♗xg5 15 hxg5 f4 16 ♗h3 ♖xe3 17 ♕h2.

13 ♕f3

In fact 13 ♘h3 0-0-0 14 ♗f4 ♗d6 15 ♕h2 ♘f8 16 0-0-0 ♘e6 17 ♗xd6 ♖xd6 18 ♗c4 ♘e7 19 ♘f4 ♘xf4 20 ♕xf4 ♖dd8 21 ♕xc7+ ♔xc7 22 c3 ♖he8 23 ♘c5 ♘c8 24 ♘d3 ♘d6 25 ♗b3 ♖e3 26 ♘f4 ♖de8 27 ♖hg1 ♖8e7 28 ♖df1 ♘e4 29 ♗d1 ♔d6 30 ♗f3 c5 31 dxc5+ ♔xc5 32 ♘g2 ♖d3 33 ♘f4 ♖d8 34 ♖d1 ♖ed7 35 ♖xd7 ♖xd7 36 ♖d1 ♖xd1+ 37 ♔xd1 ♘d6 38 ♔c2 a5 39 a4 ♔b6 40 ♔d3 ♗c7 41 ♔d4 ♘c8 42 b4 axb4 43 cxb4 ♘e7 44 a5 f6 45 gxf6 gxf6 46 ♔c5 ♗f7 47 b5 ♔c8 48 b6 1-0 (Bronstein-Beliavsky, Yerevan 1975) was the original game to conceive the 10 f5 exf5 11 g5 concept, but overall I

144

personally consider the main game to be more convincing.

13...♗d6 14 ♘e2 f4

One can see why Black jettisons this extra pawn as after, say, 14...0-0-0 15 ♗f4 it's not clear whether the g6-bishop will ever see the light of day again. Nevertheless, returning the pawn only seems to cause different problems and White soon takes advantage of the newly opened h3-c8 diagonal.

15 c4 c5 16 ♗xf4 ♘e7 17 0-0-0

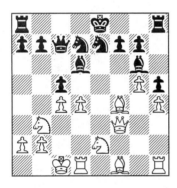

Stopping here to assess the position, White, partly due to his extra centre pawn, simply has the freer game. Black's knights are defensively placed and he has to sweat over where to place his king; a problem that, as it turns out, he never resolves.

17...♗xf4+ 18 ♕xf4 ♕xf4+ 19 ♘xf4 cxd4 20 ♖e1

20 ♘xd4 would have left White with a superior position, but this e-file pin is too attractive to pass up.

20...♔d8 21 ♘xd4 a6 22 ♗h3 ♖c8 23 b3 b5 24 ♘fe6+ fxe6 25

♘xe6+ ♔e8 26 ♘xg7+ ♔f7 1-0

Or 26...♔d8 27 ♖d1. Both knights would now drop after 27 ♖hf1+ and so without waiting for the inevitable, Black throws in the towel.

Points

Anatoly 3
Boris 1
Chris 2
Dan 0
Elizabeth 10

Solution 4-9

A careful analysis of this position confirms that Black is struggling although the following high-level encounter ended prematurely:

Adams-Granda Zuniga
Madrid 1998

22...♖fe8?? 23 ♕xe8+! ♖xe8 24 ♖xa4 1-0

Yes, after 24...♖xe1 25 ♖xd4 White would be a good piece up.

Let's check out some alternatives:

a) 22...♕d7? 23 ♖d1! ♕f5 24

♗h6 and White wins the exchange.

b) 22...♛c6? 23 ♗b4! (this is the strongest continuation although both 23 ♗h6 and 23 ♗g5 have a certain appeal too) 23...♖de8 (23...♖fe8? fails to 24 ♖xd4 ♖xe2 25 ♖xd8+ when White nets more than enough pieces for the queen; however, Black has to do something to lure White away from simple c-file action) 24 ♛d2 ♖xe1 25 ♛xe1 ♛d5 26 ♛d2. Now it is the bishop that is pinned, with 26...♖d8 27 ♖xd4 ♛xd4 28 ♛xd4 ♖xd4 29 ♗xc5 ♖a4 30 a3 being a hopeless cause for Black.

c) 22...♗xf2+ 23 ♛xf2!. Okay, Dan may have a point about 23 ♔xf2 ♛xa2 but that is irrelevant! White's bishop on f1 protects the c4-rook whilst Black, who is already a piece down, now finds both his queen and knight attacked.

By a process of elimination, the truth is that 22...♛xa2! 23 ♗h6 (or similarly 23 ♗b4 ♛xe2 24 ♖xe2 ♘e6) 23...♛xe2 24 ♖xe2 ♘e6 25 ♗xf8 ♔xf8

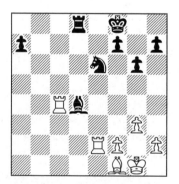

is Black's best hope. At least he has a pawn for the exchange and the powerful dark-squared bishop provides him with some reasonable drawing chances. Pretty tough!

Points
Anatoly 3
Boris 3
Chris 1
Dan 1
Elizabeth 10

Solution 4-10

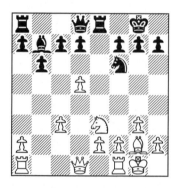

I've got to say that I'm not too impressed with 15...h5?! as Black is hardly well placed to initiate any sort of attack. This premature advance only serves to weaken Black's position.

That aside, this is frankly a high scoring question as all of the suggestions are reasonable. However, taking everything into consideration (and I'm not saying that it leads to a winning position), one can't help but be drawn to the following continuation:

Razuvaev-Tiviakov
Rostov 1993
15...Ξxe3! 16 fxe3 d6

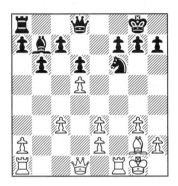

Taking stock, let's consider just what Black has got for his sacrificed material:

1) The pleasure of wrecking White's pawn structure. In particular, White's doubled e-pawns are going to be natural future targets.

2) In contrast, Black's own pawn structure is rock solid and the fixed nature of the d-pawns works in favour of his rather than his opponent's bishop.

3) As White no longer has an f-pawn, the e5-square now officially becomes an outpost. Any black piece would look good there and for now the knight is itching to do so.

17 Ξd4 ♘d7

I was always impressed by this main game. However, 15...Ξxe3!? has apparently scored 100 per cent in practice and arguably more convincing still is the more recent 17...♛e7 18 Ξf4 Ξe8 19 e4 ♘d7 20 Ξaf1 ♘e5 21 ♛a4 a5 22 ♛b5 ♗c8

23 c4 ♗d7 24 ♛b3 h6 25 Ξ4f2 Ξa8 26 ♛c3 a4 27 Ξb1 Ξa5 28 ♛d4 Ξc5 29 Ξb4 ♛g5 30 Ξf1 h5 31 ♛f2 ♛d2 32 ♛e1 ♛xa2 0-1 (Samarin-Chernyshov, Briansk 1995).

18 Ξf4 ♛e7 19 Ξaf1 ♘e5 20 ♗e4 Ξf8 21 ♗d3 ♗c8 22 ♛e4 g6 23 Ξf6 ♔g7 24 c4?!

I'm not too keen on this move as it reduces the scope of the light-squared bishop. Probably 24 ♛h4, intending to meet 24...Ξe8 with 25 ♗b5 or even 24 h4, was a better alternative.

24...♗d7 25 h4 ♛xf6!?

Certainly not forced but a fantastic concept nevertheless. With such a superior pawn structure Black is happy to play with a rook and a piece against a queen.

26 Ξxf6 ♔xf6 27 ♛d4 Ξe8 28 ♔f2 ♔g7 29 ♔e1 f6 30 ♔d2 ♘g4 31 e4

Undesirable bearing in mind the presence of the light-squared bishop, but there was no other way to secure this pawn.

31...♘e5 32 ♛c3 Ξe7 33 ♛a3 a5

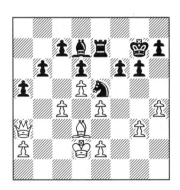

Simply put, there are no chinks in Black's armour.

34 ♕b2 ♘f7 35 ♗c2 ♖e5 36 ♕a3 ♔f8 37 ♗a4 ♗g4 38 ♕d3 ♔e7 39 c5?

This attempt at gaining some activity doesn't work out well, but White probably spotted Black's plan of manoeuvring his bishop to g6 (in order to mop up the e4-pawn) and decided not to hang around!

39...dxc5 40 ♕b5 ♘d6 41 ♕c6 ♔d8 42 ♗c2 ♗c8 43 ♕a8

White works hard with this queen from now on, but the rest of the game is a painful experience for him!

43...g5! 44 ♕c6?! gxh4 45 gxh4 ♖h5 46 e5 fxe5 47 ♕a4 e4 48 ♕b3 ♗b7 49 ♕c3 ♗xd5 50 ♕f6+ ♔d7 51 a4 ♔c6 52 ♕e7 ♔b7 53 ♔c3 ♗c6 54 ♔b2 c4 55 ♔c3 ♘c8! 56 ♕f6 ♖c5 57 ♕h6 ♘e7 58 ♕xh7 ♘d5+ 59 ♔d4 c3 60 ♗xe4 ♘b4 61 ♗g6 ♗xa4 62 h5 c2 63 ♗xc2 ♗xc2 64 ♕f7 a4 65 h6 a3 0-1

Points

Anatoly 8

Boris 1

Chris 10

Dan 7

Elizabeth 8

Solutions To Test Five

Solution 5-1

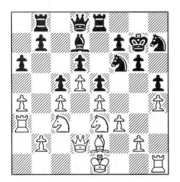

This was one of my own games and each of the panel's suggestions at least crossed my mind. Well in truth I didn't care too much for, say, 19 a5 ♕e7 20 ♘a4 ♗xa4 21 ♖xa4 b5 22 axb6 ♖xb6 (for that matter the immediate 19...b5 should guarantee Black some b-file action too). As Black is struggling for any activity, it seems a shame to hand him some on a plate and thus I would prefer the Boris idea to the Anatoly school of thought.

However, rather than donating Black the c5-square, I feel that White should be content to hold the queenside, concentrating his efforts on the kingside instead. The drawback of 19 0-0 ♕e7 20 f4?! exf4 21 ♖xf4 is that it con-

cedes the e5-square. Black would ideally like to plonk a knight there, but for the time being 21...♕e5 leaves the black queen on a dominating post.

Bearing in mind the attractive prospect of a kingside attack, the most obvious plan is that of Chris's, but contemplating the situation at the time, I soon began to have my doubts. Observe, for example, 19 g4 b6 20 ♘cd1? hxg4 21 fxg4 ♘xe4, but that aside, in general I wasn't sure that I would be able to force ...hxg4. If I couldn't then I would eventually have to employ my f-pawn anyway (in order to make serious progress) and without the support of a pawn on g3 that would entail giving away the e5-square.

As it happens I am more than satisfied with the game continuation:

Ward-Grubert
Politiken Cup, Copenhagen 2003
19 g3 ♕e7 20 ♗d3 ♘f8 21 ♕g2 ♔h7 22 ♔d2 ♗c8 23 ♖aa1 ♘8d7 24 ♔c2 b6 25 ♖hf1 ♘f8 26 ♖f2

Admittedly the game soon came to rather an abrupt end. I had it in mind to double rooks and break with f4 (with e4-e5 eventually coming should ...exf4 gxf4 be Black's reaction).

26...♕d7 27 ♖af1 ♕h3 28 ♕g1 ♖b7 29 f4 exf4 30 ♖xf4

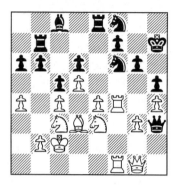

Okay, so I lied! I did give away the e5-square after all, but of course given the way that Black has arranged his pieces in the interim, that pales into insignificance beside the problems now experienced on the f-file.

30...♘8d7 31 ♖1f2 1-0

Yes, of course 31 ♖xf6 was more than adequate but with the queen-trapping 32 ♗f1 now on the cards, Black must jettison a whole piece.

Points
Anatoly 1
Boris 4
Chris 4
Dan 3
Elizabeth 10

Solution 5-2

Probably 11...g5 was over-ambitious but White must be a little careful as he still has development of his own to complete. As an example, even 12 ♘f3 ♗g7 13 0-0 f6 isn't so clear as the white centre that has required a lot of moves to build up comes under immediate pressure. Similarly, although 12 h4 g4 13 h5 is standard in order to prevent ...h5 and fix the g-pawn as a target, the natural 13...f6 then puts the cat amongst the pigeons. Indeed, White must be careful that things don't backfire and after 12 b5 b6!? 13 bxc6 ♘xc6 the position has opened up to his detriment.

I'm really not impressed by 12 f4 g4, which leaves Black in full control of f5 and White struggling to get his king's knight out. So, by a process of elimination we have a ruthless exhibition:

Kasparov-Shirov
Russia versus the World, Moscow 2002
12 g4!
Garry ensures that Black's g-pawn will only have a short shelf life. His intention is to trade that

one but to bag the h-pawn free of charge and everything goes pretty much according to plan.

12...♗g6

Arguably 12...♗e4!? 13 f3 ♗g6 is more accurate but 14 h4 should feature anyway.

13 h4! ♗g7

Upon 13...gxh4 14 ♖xh4, barring the extremely undesirable 14...♘g8, the h-pawn would soon drop.

14 hxg5 hxg5 15 ♖xh8+ ♗xh8 16 ♗xg5

Basically White has won a pawn for nothing and arguably the world's greatest ever player converts with relative ease.

**16...a5 17 b5 ♘xc5 18 ♗f6!
♗xf6 19 exf6 ♘g8 20 dxc5 d4
21 ♘f3! dxc3 22 ♕xc3 ♕f4 23
g5! ♖d8 24 bxc6 bxc6 25 ♖d1
♖xd1+ 26 ♗xd1 ♕e4+ 27 ♔f1
♗h5 28 ♕b3 ♕f4 29 ♕b7 ♕c4+
30 ♔e1 1-0**

As there are some very plausible answers I'm going to award quite a lot of points for this one.

Points

Anatoly 10
Boris 5
Chris 4
Dan 2
Elizabeth 5

Solution 5-3

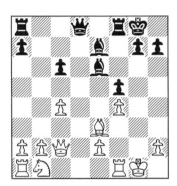

I clearly have to make this one a high scoring question too as between them our panel encompass most of the position's critical features. As Black is a pawn down and White still lags behind in the development stakes, personally I would recommend speedy action. Therefore I'm not so keen on Anatoly's idea. Regarding Boris's suggestion, Black's pawn structure after 17...g5 18 hxg5 ♗xg5 19 ♗xg5 ♕xg5+ 20 ♔h1 isn't great but the most annoying things are that White has a rook coming to the g-file and it is not so easy to get the light-squared bishop on the long diagonal.

Dan's concept is very logical, whilst 17...♖e8 also has a certain appeal. Nevertheless, although one could argue that it is down to a matter of taste, I'm awarding the top score to Chris. Take a look at the following game:

Vukic-Hulak
Zlatibor 1989
17...♖f6! 18 ♘d2 c5!

Black opens up the a8-h1 diagonal with the intention of manoeuvring his bishop there via c8.

19 ♘f3 ♕e8 20 ♖fd1 ♗c8 21 ♗d2 ♗b7 22 ♗c3 ♗e4 23 ♕d2 ♖h6 24 ♕d7 ♕g6+

Obviously Black is not interested in a queen trade bearing in mind the strength of the g- and h-file attack.

25 ♔f2 ♗xf3

Only now with a clear path ahead does Black concede one of his bishops.

26 exf3

Observe 26 ♕xe7 ♖xh2+ 27 ♔xf3 ♕g2+ 28 ♔e3 ♕xe2 mate.

26...♖xh2+ 27 ♔e3 ♖e8

The white king has jumped out of the frying pan and into the fire!

28 ♕d5+ ♔h8 29 ♖g1 ♗f6+

29...♖h4+ 30 ♔d3 ♖g2 31 ♖xg2 ♕xg2, threatening...♕e2+ and...♖d8, also would have been pretty terminal.

30 ♔d3 ♖he2 31 ♗e5 ♗xe5 32 ♖xg6 ♗xf4 33 ♖e6 ♖8xe6 34 ♕xc5 ♖6e3+ 0-1

Points
Anatoly 3
Boris 2
Chris 10
Dan 7
Elizabeth 6

Solution 5-4

I was at this Danish tournament recently and I can tell you that the Ex-Soviet grandmaster was not a happy bunny after the following encounter:

Beliavsky-Høi
Politiken Cup, Copenhagen 2003
36...♘g3+?! 37 hxg3 hxg3 38 ♔g1 ♕h6 39 ♖h8+?? ♔xh8 40 ♕xf6+ ♔g8 0-1

The perpetual didn't appear and mate is inevitable.

Now let us get to the truth of the matter. Firstly, 37 ♔g1 ♘xf1 38 ♔xf1 h3 is if anything slightly better for Black but White should accept the sacrifice.

After 37 hxg3 hxg3 I'm afraid that Elizabeth's 38 ♗d3?? walks into 38...♕c1+! (an improvement on 38...♕h6+) 39 ♕g1 ♕h6+. However, in the game continuation of 38 ♔g1 ♕h6 White should of course employ 39 ♗e2!. The white king doesn't actually have to use this e2-square to escape as after 39...♕h2+ (there is no future either for 39...♕c1+ 40 ♗d1) 40 ♔f1 ♕h1+ White can retreat his queen. There is a little untangling to do but 41 ♕g1 ♕h6 42 ♖a1 does the business. Dan is spot on because 38 ♗e2 provides a defence that should transpose to our main variation.

Given the time trouble conditions of the game, actually 36...♘g3+ was a reasonable practical try. It should have lost but in this pressure situation the tricky Danish IM was rewarded with an impressive scalp.

Points
Anatoly 0
Boris 0
Chris 1
Dan 10
Elizabeth 0

Solution 5-5

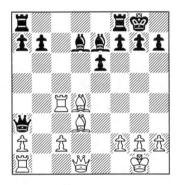

Take a look at the following:

Ibraev-Sergeev
St Petersburg 2003
18 ♗xh7+! ♔xh7 19 ♕h5+ ♔g8 20 ♗xg7! f5
Note 20...♔xg7 21 ♖g4+ ♔f6 22 ♕g5 mate.
21 ♗e5 ♖f6 22 ♖h4 1-0
(see following diagram)
With that in mind I have no option but to award Boris's solution ten points.
Although 18 ♗xg7 ♔xg7 19 ♕g4+ ♔h8 20 ♕d4+ ♔g8 21 ♕xd7 is favourable for White, it is hardly as emphatic.

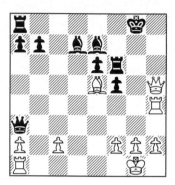

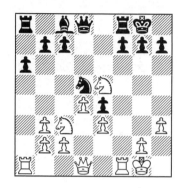

It is true that 18 ♕h5 g6? 19 ♕h6 f6 20 ♗xg6! hxg6 21 ♕xg6+ ♔h8 22 ♗c5, bringing ♖h4+ into the equation, would be an impressive way to win but 18...f5 is a far superior defence. On the other hand, 18 ♕g4 can be met adequately by 18...g6.

As for 18 ♗e4, well I suppose as White also still threatens 19 ♗xh7+ (!),he is still doing well. Nevertheless, it is 18 ♗xh7+! for me.

Points

Anatoly 3
Boris 10
Chris 4
Dan 1
Elizabeth 2

Solution 5-6

I'm going to break with tradition here by supplying the whole game because the following encounter has got to have had the most insipid opening that I have ever seen (I was sitting on the next board) between two Grandmasters!

Short-Stefanova
British League 2003
1 e4 e5 2 ♘f3 ♘c6 3 ♗c4 ♗c5 4 ♘c3 ♘f6 5 d3 a6 6 ♗e3 d6 7 h3 ♗xe3 8 fxe3

Fast improving young English GM Luke McShane would no doubt have called this baby chess. Now, though, White has a half-open f-file to use, and use it he does!
8...♘a5 9 ♗b3 0-0 10 0-0 ♘xb3 11 axb3 d5 12 ♘xe5 dxe4 13 d4 ♘d5? 14 ♖xf7! ♖xf7 15 ♘xf7 ♘xc3

This is forced as Black cannot contemplate 15...♔xf7? 16 ♕h5+ ♔e6 17 ♕e5+.
16 ♘xd8 ♘xd1 17 ♖xd1 a5

Perhaps some might have resisted playing Nigel's temporary sacrifice just in case the knight got trapped behind enemy lines. Certainly 17...♗g4 18 hxg4 ♖xd8 is a minor piece trade that leaves a winning rook and pawn ending, and bearing in mind 17...♔f8 18 ♖f1+, Short's calculations no doubt informed him that the steed was always going to find its way out.

**18 ♖f1 a4 19 bxa4 ♖xa4 20 ♖f7!
♖c4 21 c3 b5 22 ♖e7 ♔f8 23
♖xe4 b4 24 cxb4 ♖xb4 25 ♘e6+
♗xe6 26 ♖xe6**

So we get a rook ending anyway which the English Grandmaster duly converts.

**26...♖xb2 27 ♖e5 ♔f7 28 ♔h2
♖b3 29 ♔g3 c5? 30 dxc5 ♖c3 31
♔f4 ♔f6 32 g4 h6 33 h4 ♖c4+
34 e4 ♖c3 35 g5+ hxg5+ 36
hxg5+ ♔f7 37 ♖d5 ♔e6 38 ♖d6+
♔e7 39 ♖g6 ♖xc5 40 ♖xg7+ ♔e6
41 ♔g4 ♖c4 42 ♔h5 ♖xe4 43
♖a7 ♖e1 44 g6 ♖h1+ 45 ♔g5
♖h2 46 ♖f7 ♖h1 47 ♖f2 ♔e7 48
g7 ♖g1+ 49 ♔h6 ♖h1+ 50 ♔g6
♖g1+ 51 ♔h7 ♖h1+ 52 ♔g8 ♖a1
53 ♖h2 1-0**

Yes, I'm going to award full marks to Anatoly although on positional grounds the ideas of Chris and Dan look reasonable too. Note that 14 ♘xf7? ♖xf7 15 ♖xf7 ♘xc3 is more of a losing try and Elizabeth's suggestion is out of charac-

ter and poor. After 14 ♘xe4?
♘xe3 15 ♕h5 ♕xd4! White is forced to relinquish further material and go on the defensive.

Points

Anatoly 10
Boris 0
Chris 5
Dan 5
Elizabeth 0

Solution 5-7

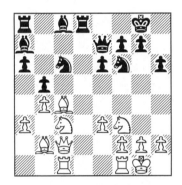

If you think that I am mean then you are going to hate me even more after seeing the correct continuation here:

Aronian-Jakovenko

World Junior Championship, Goa 2002

15 ♘xb5!! axb5 16 ♗xb5 ♘xb4

The point is that White had correctly calculated 16...♘b8 17 ♕xc8!
♖xc8 18 ♖xc8+ ♔h7 19 ♗d3+ g6 20
♗xf6 ♕xf6 21 ♗e4 as leaving him with a significant material advantage.

155

17 axb4 ♖b8

Perhaps Black should have chanced his arm with 17...♕xb4 although 18 ♕c7! ♖f8 (or 18...♗d7? 19 ♗xf6) 19 ♗xf6 gxf6 20 ♖b1 ♕c5 21 ♕g3+ ♔h8 22 ♕f4 is hardly an attractive prospect.

18 ♘e5!

A useful move that, because of the fork on c6, helps White retain his extra b-pawn and thus ultimately aids him in winning the game.

18...♗b7 19 ♕a4 ♗e4 20 ♖c4 ♗d5 21 ♘c6 ♗xc6 22 ♗xc6

The pawn is still there and White has the bishop pair too. Essentially it's game over!

22...♘d5 23 ♖g4 e5 24 b5 f5 25 ♖c4 ♘b6 26 ♕b4 ♕e6 27 ♖cc1 ♖f8 28 ♕c3 ♘d7 29 ♖fd1 1-0

Just two pawns alone wouldn't be enough for a piece, particularly in the middlegame and hence I must reject the Boris approach. As for the others, well take your pick. I'm sure that I have tried pretty much all of the panel's three bishop retreats in similar positions and with

no obvious bias here I must agree that that decision is down to a matter of taste.

Points

Anatoly 5
Boris 0
Chris 5
Dan 10
Elizabeth 5

Solution 5-8

Porreca-Bronstein
Belgrade 1954

11...♗g8!?

It was Jon Speelman who described this game and move to me around our table at the Wood Green celebration dinner. This move sounded bizarre to me at the time (particularly after a few glasses of wine!) and it still looks rather odd. However, not content to just bow to Jon's greater understanding of the Caro Kann, I felt compelled to get to grips with this amazing retreat.

First of all, one should accept

that the pawn sacrifice 11...0-0-0? 12 ♗xf7 is not a playable continuation due to the massive hole conceded on e6. Also, although it looks obvious, the natural 11...e6? walks straight into 12 ♗xe6! fxe6 13 ♘xe6 with an extremely dangerous initiative.

At the end of the day, the justification for 11...♗g8!? is that Black has a problem to solve. If he can simply put one piece on an awkward square in order to help him progress then he can always return it later when the danger has passed. As it turns out, that is exactly what happens:

12 ♘d3 e6 13 ♗f4 ♗d6 14 ♗xd6 ♕xd6 15 ♘f5 ♕f8

Backwards again but only to deal with another threat: this time to the g7-pawn.

16 ♕f3 0-0-0

With the e-pawn now unpinned, White must do something about his knight.

17 ♘g3 ♗h7 18 a4 ♗xd3

Evidently Black deemed it easier to remove this knight than to wander into the complexity of the continuation 18...♘b6 19 ♗b3 ♖xd4 20 ♘e5.

19 ♗xd3 ♕d6

And normal service has been resumed! Of course it would be outrageous for me to suggest that Black is winning now but he has a rock solid position and can continue the game without any silly-looking pieces.

20 a5 a6 21 ♖a3 g5 22 h5 ♕f4 23 ♕e2 ♔c7 24 c3 ♖he8 25 ♘e4 ♘xe4 26 ♕xe4 ♕xe4 27 ♗xe4 ♘f6 28 ♗f3 g4 29 ♗d1 ♖g8 30 ♖e5 ♖d5 31 ♖a4 ♖g5 32 ♗b3 ♖dxe5 33 dxe5 ♘d7 34 ♗d1 ♘xe5 35 ♖e4 ♖xh5 36 ♗xg4 ♘xg4 37 ♖xg4 ♖xa5 38 ♖g7 ♖f5 39 g4 ♖f6 40 ♔g2 ♔d6 41 ♔g3 e5 42 ♖g8 ♔d5 0-1

Though certainly deserving of some points, Anatoly's 11...♘b6 12 ♗b3 ♘bd5 13 ♘xd5 ♘xd5 14 ♕f3 e6 15 c4 still seems to encourage a certain amount of pressure in the centre, whilst 11...g5 12 hxg5 hxg5 13 ♘fh5 leaves Black with some kingside weaknesses.

Points
Anatoly 6
Boris 2
Chris 10
Dan 0
Elizabeth 4

Solution 5-9

After both 50...♖h7 51 ♖b1 and 50...a4 51 ♗a3! I can't see any obvious way in for the black rook. Note that by keeping the bishop on a3, White doesn't need to give his opponent the opportunity to offload his a-pawn.

At a glance one may be forgiven thinking that, not for the first time, Dan hasn't exactly got his head screwed on properly. However, although I'm not always a fan of old games, one must give credit where it is due (i.e. 10 points!) for the following:

Kmoch-Nimzowitsch
Bad Niendorf 1927
50...♖b4!! 51 cxb4

After 51 ♗xb4 axb4 52 cxb4 ♔b5 the passed b- and c-pawns will win the day. Meanwhile, ignoring Black's plan is hopeless, e.g. 51 ♔f3 ♖a4 52 ♔g2 ♖a1 and the a-pawn will go marching on.
51...a4!

The important move. As well as

52...c3 Black now has 52...♔b5 in mind, when the three passed pawns can advance at their leisure.
52 b5+ ♔xb5 53 ♗a3 c3 54 ♖b1

After 54 ♔f3 cxb2 55 ♗xb2 Black easily dissolves the dark-squared blockade with 55...♔b4.
54...♔c4 55 f4 ♔xd4 56 ♔f2 ♔c4 57 ♔e1 d4

Yes, as a fourth passed pawn appears Black's own bishop is still yet to move!
58 ♔e2 ♔d5 59 ♔f3 ♗b7 60 ♖e1 ♔c4+ 61 ♔f2 b2 62 f5 exf5 63 e6 ♗c6 0-1

I'm all for zugzwang and all that, but I'm afraid that Elizabeth is asking a bit much as there are too many squares available to the white bishop.

Points
Anatoly 0
Boris 3
Chris 3
Dan 10
Elizabeth 2

Solution 5-10

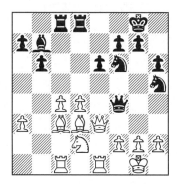

Apart from 22...e5?, which just seems to lose a pawn to 23 ♕xe5!, all of our panel's suggestions are pretty reasonable. However, I can't help thinking that after the likes of 22...♘g4 23 ♕xf4 ♘xf4 24 ♗f1, as the black knights will be rebuffed, the presence of the bishop pair probably leaves White with a slight edge. The same then could easily be said of 22...♕b8 23 g3 and 22...♖c7 23 g3, so I have no hesitation in giving maximum points to Dan's suggestion:

Aleksandrov-Adams
Bled Olympiad 2002
22...♗xg2! 23 ♔xg2 ♘g4 24 ♕h3?

Preferable variations from a White point of view were 24 ♕xf4 ♘xf4+ 25 ♔g3 ♘xd3 26 ♔xg4

♘xf2+! 27 ♔f3 ♘d3 or 24 ♕f3 ♕xh2+ 25 ♔f1 ♘xf2! 26 ♖e3! (guarding the g3-square) 26...♘xd3 27 ♖xd3 e5!. Nevertheless, in the former case the endgame favours Black and in the latter he retains three pawns and a reasonable initiative for the piece. This makes 22...♗xg2 a better option than any of the others.

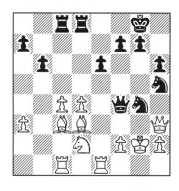

24...♕xf2+ 25 ♔h1 ♕xe1+! 26 ♖xe1 ♘f2+ 27 ♔g2 ♘xh3 28 ♔xh3 ♘f4+ 29 ♔g3 ♘xd3 30 ♖e3 ♘c1 31 ♗b2 ♘a2! 32 ♖b3 b5 33 c5 ♖b8 34 ♘e4 b4 35 a4 ♘c3 0-1

Points
Anatoly 5
Boris 1
Chris 5
Dan 10
Elizabeth 5

Marking Scheme and Scorechart

	Test 1	Test 2	Test 3	Test 4	Test 5
1					
2					
3					
4					
5					
6					
7					
8					
9					
10					
Total					

0-20 Usually at this point I will make some sarcastic remark about how you would have been just as well off guessing! However, because there were on average 22 points on offer per question and you have scored on average 2 or less, then the cold harsh truth is that you have performed poorly.

21-40 You most likely didn't rely on the laws of probability or at least not for all ten questions! Not bad, but not good either!

41-60 Now we're starting to get somewhere! You are clearly an experienced campaigner and, demonstrate a reasonable chess understanding.

61-80 Pretty impressive. Many strong players have confirmed that there were some tough cookies here and you have negotiated them well. Good luck in your quest for the IM or even GM title that should be your ambition.

81-100 Superb! These were high-level questions and you have demonstrated that you were definitely up to the challenge. Depending on where you were in this score band, I would rate you somewhere between a very strong club player and (nearing the 100%) a Grandmaster. Congratulations!